giada's feel good food

Giada's FEEL GOOD FOOD

my healthy recipes and secrets

giada de laurentiis

CLARKSON POTTER/PUBLISHERS
New York

Library of Congress Cataloging-in-Publication Data
De Laurentiis, Giada.
Giada's feel good food / Giada De Laurentiis.
Includes index.
1. Cooking. I. Title.
TX714.D423 2013
641.5—dc23   2013004298

ISBN 978-0-307-98720-4
eISBN 978-0-307-98721-1

Printed in Hong Kong

Book and jacket design by Rae Ann Spitzenberger
Book and jacket photographs by Amy Neunsinger

10 9 8 7 6 5 4 3 2 1

First Edition

To my daughter, Jade, who
inspires me daily to stay creatively
hungry; to my fans, who always
keep my heart so full; and to my
brother, Dino, my daily inspiration
to savor every bite of life.

contents

introduction

The number one question I'm asked by fans of my television shows and cookbooks is, "How do you stay so trim?" This book is my answer. It's a personal look into how I keep my body and my mind in a happy and healthy balance!

But I want to get one important thing straight right now: This is *not* a diet book. I don't live my life on a diet; I just don't believe in them for me. They are tough to stick to and encourage a sense of deprivation or missing out, resulting in roller-coaster weight loss and gain—and the mood swings that come along with that. I'm not a yo-yo and I can't put my mind or body through that. Instead, I have adopted a balanced way of cooking, eating, and living that works for me and my family. This didn't happen overnight, or by sitting down and scribbling a bunch of rules to follow, but rather over time, by tuning in to my body and what makes me run the smoothest and tuning out what doesn't.

When I was younger, I was completely addicted to chocolate and sugar. I relied on them to give me an energy boost throughout the day. In fact, I would eat less "regular" food in order to leave room for dessert! If it was coated in chocolate, it was for me: chocolate-covered almonds, graham crackers, cookies . . . chocolate anything, really. I put tons of sugar in my coffee and iced tea. I was also a fan of the Italian custom of dipping sugar cubes in espresso and sucking on them, going through several cubes at a time.

And when I was young, this didn't seem to affect me much. Sure, I had some dips here and there in my energy level throughout the day, but I had more energy in general and didn't see a huge downside to this lifestyle.

When I became pregnant with Jade, however, everything changed. I was responsible for this little life inside of me and I took the saying "eating for two" to heart. My body needed—and my baby deserved—better. This made me rethink my whole lifestyle.

So I started making little adjustments here and there, changing bit by bit. I cut down on my sugar intake and started being more mindful of what I was eating in general. I ate more, which makes sense because I was pregnant, but that meant more vegetables, protein, and whole grains and a lot less sweet stuff. I started buying organic ingredients and produce, trying to limit the pesticides and chemicals in my system as much as possible. And guess what, I began to feel better—even better than better. I felt great. Pregnant! And once Jade was born, I didn't revert back to my old habits. Jade has taught me so many things, but I like to think of this new lifestyle as her first lesson, her first gift to me.

I can honestly say that, in my forties, I am healthier than I was in my twenties or thirties.

I continue to tweak and improve upon it, always looking to make healthy adjustments, but I have to say I feel better than I ever have. I have more energy than ever before, which is how I keep up with my crazy busy schedule! I can honestly say that, in my forties, I am healthier than I was in my twenties or thirties. I sleep better. I feel happier. Jade changed it for me and I am grateful for all the joys she brings me. I knew there would be many; this was just an unexpected bonus!

I still love chocolate—that'll never change, and I don't want it to! I still eat it often, only now I do so in moderation. It's one of my pleasures, a little treat that makes me smile.

That brings me to my number one philosophy on eating: Eat a little of everything, but not a lot of anything. It's such a simple idea but it took me a long time to embrace it fully. I don't believe in deprivation; it just fuels cravings and creates a vicious cycle of negative feelings. On the other side, overindulgence with any one thing just dulls your taste for it, leaving you eating more of it, trying to get that same pleasure, which isn't a good thing.

I'm not saying you can't eat burgers. You just can't eat them five days a week! The good news is that when you make smarter choices, your taste buds will change. Your body will tell you what it needs to run best and your cravings will reflect this.

I now really gravitate toward whole grains and keep an eye on how much wheat I consume. Being mindful also of how much meat, fat, and salt I consume has led me to discover and fall in love with many kinds of whole grains, including quinoa, hominy, and kamut. Replacing foods that are high on the glycemic index (GI)—that is, foods high in refined sugar and refined complex carbohydrates, like white bread—with foods with less sugar and more fiber has made a huge difference in my energy levels. Low-GI foods are absorbed more slowly by the body and keep you going longer. These days, I opt for light agave nectar instead of white sugar to sweeten my drinks. (You can even buy agave packets to take with you on the go.) It's still sweet but it doesn't give you a sugar high—and the resulting crash. You'll find nondairy milks in my fridge at home—from almond to coconut—to replace some of the regular dairy. In writing down many of my favorite dishes for this book, I realized that many are gluten-free, vegetarian, and even vegan (entirely free of animal products), and I thought, *this born and bred Italian has come a long way!* But it's great because this way I can still eat a bit of everything—and enjoy it all!

Another key to my lifestyle is that I eat many times over the course of a day. While breakfast is absolutely the most important meal of the day, you can forget that old rule about not snacking between meals. Five smaller meals a day are so much better for you; they are easier for you to digest than three big ones, which makes for a happy metabolism! Instead of the highs and lows and feeling like you're starved or stuffed, you stay much more even-keeled throughout the day. Your body adapts to this routine and begins to work much more efficiently. This will become part of your schedule, and to help you get there, this book has great grab-and-go snack recipes. You can make them ahead and then stash them in your bag for a midmorning or afternoon pick-me-up (see page 134).

Portions: You have to pay attention to them. A steak the size of your head is not a single portion. Many people don't know what a real serving size is because it is not what we were taught

IVORY, RED, AND MULTICOLOR QUINOA

growing up (though thankfully that is changing!). Four ounces of protein—meat, fish, or tofu, for example—is the equivalent of your palm (your hand minus the fingers) and about the same thickness, too; it's a good guide to aim for.

Vegetables, legumes, and fruits—all packed with fiber—make up the majority of what I eat. When I want pasta (which is often!), I usually tend to have it at lunch so I have more time to use its fuel during the day. At dinnertime, I pack in a little more protein to hold me until morning and I always make sure to give myself plenty of time to digest before I go to bed; I aim for three hours or so before falling asleep.

After I've been traveling a lot—and especially if eating the way I prefer to has been challenging on a trip—I turn to juices and smoothies to help rewire my body, kick jet lag, and get myself back into my routine. I've dedicated a whole chapter in this book to juices and smoothies because they taste amazing and are great almost any time of day. I love how you can pick a flavor to match what you're craving, whether it is something sweet or something green—or maybe both! If I'm feeling truly lethargic, I might even go on a juice cleanse for up to a couple of days (see page 54).

Here's another revelation: I will never be a gym person. I am just not a runner. The idea of being strapped to a treadmill every day is my worst nightmare . . . and that's okay! I like walks along the beach and my morning yoga, both of which keep me centered and happy. Todd and I also love to paddle-board out on the ocean together. You definitely have to use your core muscles to stay on the board! Exercise is important, but I also think it is important that you enjoy it. Exercise keeps your energy flowing and the blood

You can forget that old rule about not snacking between meals.

SPICED COCKTAIL NUTS, PAGE 144

circulating; it stokes the inner fire. But, I truly believe that great health starts with what you put in your mouth.

Because of that, you'll notice that this is the first cookbook of mine where you'll find a nutritional breakdown for each recipe. While personally I do not count calories or carbs, I know that many people do and find it helpful—and I want to open up these recipes to as many people as possible. Some dishes have more or fewer calories—or grams of fat or milligrams of sodium; I believe in overall balance. It's all about finding what works for you and sticking to it—and knowing what is actually in what you are eating is a great start. You'll also see that I've called out vegetarian, vegan, gluten-free, and dairy-free recipes. I wanted to give you many alternatives to cook meals that make you and your family feel good.

recipe icons

- (v) vegetarian
- (vg) vegan
- (gf) gluten free
- (df) dairy free

Everyone is different. Genetics made me short and small-boned. But it's not about how much you weigh or if you look as thin as someone else; it's about looking in the mirror and loving yourself. Having more energy and fewer ups and downs is half the battle in my world. I feel stable and can give my full attention to everyone and everything in my life: my daughter, my husband, my friends, my work, and myself.

Above all, give your body a bit more attention; plan your meals a little better, and your body will reward you tenfold. I promise you will smile more and you will enjoy life more because you will feel better!

This is what works for me. I hope it helps you find what works for you.

xo

Giada

a month of feel good meals

	monday	tuesday	wednesday
BREAKFAST	Breakfast Bulgur Wheat with Poached Mixed Berries	Oatmeal with Cinnamon Sugar	Chia Seed Pudding
LUNCH	Sweet Potatoes with Creamy Tofu-Lime Vinaigrette	Turkey, Kale, and Brown Rice Soup	Updated Waldorf Salad with Apple Vinaigrette
SNACK	Avocado Hummus with Crispy Pita Chips	Homemade Cranberry Nut Granola	Crispy Chickpeas
DINNER	Grilled Chicken Cutlets with Fresh Apple-Mango Chutney	Whole-Wheat Linguine with Shrimp, Asparagus, and Cherry Tomatoes	Salmon with Lemon, Capers, and Rosemary
DESSERT	Chocolate Cranberry Treats		Fruit Spring Rolls
BREAKFAST	Orange-Scented Almond and Olive Oil Muffins	Egg, Kale, and Tomato Breakfast Wraps with Hummus	Citrus Parfaits
LUNCH	Radicchio, Pear, and Arugula Salad	Quinoa Pilaf	Chicken, Mango, and Black Beans with Lime-Almond Dressing
SNACK	Double Berry Smoothie	Cinnamon Kettle Corn	Smoked Almonds
DINNER	Grilled Salmon and Pineapple with Avocado Dressing	California Turkey Chili	Grilled Herbed Tofu with Avocado Cream
DESSERT	Mini Carrot-Apple Cupcakes		
BREAKFAST	Egg White Scramble with Spicy Tomato Salsa	Vanilla, Date, Almond Smoothie with Yogurt	Chia Seed Pudding
LUNCH	Butter Lettuce and Tuna Salad with Pear Dressing	Wheat Berries with Strawberries	Shrimp and Avocado Salad
SNACK	Rosemary Cashews and Sunflower Seeds	Avocado Hummus with Crispy Pita Chips	Beet, Ginger, and Apple Juice
DINNER	Roasted Vegetables with Chipotle Cream over Crispy Pita	Sliced Pork with Citrus Slaw	Broiled Sole with Mustard-Chive Sauce
DESSERT		Chocolate Fig Bites	Peach and Blueberry Crumble
BREAKFAST	Citrus Parfaits	Breakfast Bulgur Wheat with Poached Mixed Berries	Spanish Potato Omelet
LUNCH	Artichoke Soup with Fresh Mint	Kale and Mushroom Wrap	Pita and Grilled Vegetable Panzanella
SNACK	Homemade Cranberry Nut Granola	Cinnamon Kettle Corn	Baked Kale and Sweet Potato Chips
DINNER	Swiss Chard Rolls with Wild and Brown Rice and Indian Spices	Grilled Striped Bass with Tomato and Bell Pepper Sauce	Shrimp, Avocado, and Mango Rolls
DESSERT	Chocolate Blueberry Brownies	Spiced Pumpkin-Raisin Cookies	

This menu shows you how to mix and match recipes in this book for a month of fabulous food. It's an example of delicious possibilities—ways to add flavor and variety to each day—but it is not something to be followed to the letter by everyone. You should customize this framework to meet your individual calorie and nutrient needs, adding appropriate foods as desired.

thursday	friday	saturday	sunday
Egg White Scramble with Spicy Tomato Salsa	Banana, Walnut, and Date Smoothie	Orange-Scented Almond and Olive Oil Muffins	Spanish Potato Omelet
Green Pea, Lettuce, and Fennel Soup	Quinoa, Roasted Eggplant, and Apple Salad with Cumin Vinaigrette	Whole-Wheat Orzo with Artichoke Pesto	Beet and Marinated Goat Cheese Salad
Lavash Chips with Creamy Tomato-Basil Dip	Chewy Granola Bars	Fruit Salad with Honey-Lime Syrup	Spiced Apple Chips
Lemon-Cumin Chicken with Mint and Spinach Pesto	Lentil Burgers with Lemon-Basil Mayonnaise	Christmas Seafood Salad	My Mom's Vegetable "Meatloaf" with Checca Sauce
Chocolate Muffins			
Almond Butter Strawberry Toast	Kale, Apple, and Cucumber Smoothie	Buckwheat Pancakes	Baked Fruit with Ricotta
Chicken Chopped Salad in Butter Lettuce Cups	Stuffed Bell Peppers	Roasted Tomato Soup with Halibut	Nonna's Artichokes
Roasted Red Pepper Hummus in Cucumber Cups	Spiced Cocktail Nuts	Grapefruit Mint Juice	Baked Kale and Sweet Potato Chips
Sole with Lemon-Basil Pesto	Pork Tenderloin with Honey-Mustard Sauce	Garlic-Roasted Chicken and Root Vegetables	Salmon Hand Rolls
Cantaloupe and Mint Granita	Avocado-Chocolate Mousse with Raspberries		Blueberry Frozen Yogurt
Oatmeal with Olive Oil	Strawberry-Mint Omelet	Rise-and-Shine Juice	California Tofu Hash
Farfalle with Chicken, Cremini Mushrooms, and Swiss Chard	Curried Chicken and Apple Wraps	Herbed Quinoa	Fennel, Radish, and Chive Salad
Spiced Cocktail Nuts	Fruit Salad with Honey-Lime Syrup	Popcorn with Herbes de Provence and Smoked Sea Salt	Roasted Red Pepper Hummus in Cucumber Cups
Vegetarian Chili Verde	Mahimahi with Mango-Vanilla Sauce	Southern Italian–Style Herbed Chicken	Grilled Scallops with Orange-Scented Quinoa
	Cranberry Lemon Cookies		Chocolate Blueberry Brownies
Oatmeal with Cinnamon Sugar	Kale Juice	Egg, Kale, and Tomato Breakfast Wraps with Hummus	Buckwheat Pancakes
Whole-Wheat Pearl Couscous Salad with Smoked Paprika	Chicken and Honey-Mustard Pinwheels	Quinoa with Black Beans and Hominy	Halibut Ceviche Salad with Avocado Salsa
Spinach, Ginger, and Apple Smoothie	Lavash Chips with Creamy Tomato-Basil Dip	Spiced Apple Chips	Strawberry and Spinach Smoothie with Yogurt
Baked Salmon with Arugula Salsa Verde	Stuffed Red Bell Peppers with Whole-Wheat Couscous and Avocado Sauce	Halibut with Artichoke and Olive Caponata	Whole Roasted Chicken with Vegetable Bolognese
	Vegan Chocolate Truffles		

breakfast

BUCKWHEAT PANCAKES

SPANISH POTATO OMELET

BREAKFAST BULGUR WHEAT
with Poached Mixed Berries

CHIA SEED PUDDING

ORANGE-SCENTED ALMOND
AND OLIVE OIL MUFFINS

OATMEAL with Olive Oil

OATMEAL with Cinnamon Sugar

BAKED FRUIT with Ricotta

STRAWBERRY-MINT OMELET

EGG, KALE, AND TOMATO
BREAKFAST WRAPS
with Hummus

CITRUS PARFAITS

EGG WHITE SCRAMBLE
with Spicy Tomato Salsa

ALMOND BUTTER
STRAWBERRY TOAST

CALIFORNIA TOFU HASH

1 large egg

⅔ cup organic buckwheat pancake mix, such as Arrowhead Mills

2 teaspoons plus 1 tablespoon safflower or grapeseed oil

3 tablespoons pure maple syrup

1 pint fresh raspberries

per serving: Calories 458; Protein 11g; Carbohydrates 72g; Dietary Fiber 14g; Sugar 27g; Total Fat 16g; Saturated Fat 2g; Sodium 418mg

buckwheat pancakes

These pancakes are a breakfast staple in my house because they can be made ahead and reheated in a toaster. And Jade loves them. The trick is finding things you feel good about serving your family and eating yourself and that everyone loves. Buckwheat flour is ground from a gluten-free seed and provides a nice nutty taste and great texture. (Read labels carefully if you want to go gluten-free: Some buckwheat mixes also contain wheat flour.) It keeps you going longer than white flour so you won't be hungry an hour after breakfast. These pancakes are a definite part of our weekly breakfast rotation. The sweetness of the berries is enough for me; Jade and Todd like a little extra maple syrup poured on top of them. *makes 6 pancakes; serves 2*

In a medium bowl, whisk the egg. Add the pancake mix, 2 teaspoons of the oil, 1 tablespoon of the maple syrup, and ¾ cup water. Whisk together until smooth.

Heat a nonstick pan over medium heat. Add the remaining 1 tablespoon oil. Using a ¼-cup measure, and working in batches, add the pancake batter to the pan and cook the pancakes until golden, 2 to 3 minutes per side.

Stack the pancakes on plates and serve topped with the fresh raspberries and the remaining 2 tablespoons maple syrup.

4 tablespoons extra-virgin olive oil

3 small onions, sliced

5 small Yukon Gold potatoes (1½ pounds), peeled and cut into ⅛-inch-thick rounds

1 teaspoon kosher salt

½ teaspoon freshly ground black pepper

5 large eggs, at room temperature

6 garlic cloves, chopped

4 large pimiento-stuffed olives, coarsely chopped

1 tablespoon chopped fresh thyme, plus sprigs for garnish

1 tablespoon chopped fresh flat-leaf parsley, plus sprigs for garnish

⅓ cup crumbled feta cheese

¾ cup Romesco Sauce (recipe follows)

per serving (includes sauce): Calories 324; Protein 9g; Carbohydrates 23g; Dietary Fiber 2g; Sugar 5g; Total Fat 22g; Saturated Fat 5g; Sodium 556mg

spanish potato omelet

This is a hearty, satisfying, and flavorful weekend breakfast recipe. I often make it for potluck brunches because it is great warm or at room temperature. A bright red romesco sauce—made from bell peppers seasoned with sweet-tart sherry vinegar and smoky paprika—enlivens the eggs and the plate. Served over a green salad, leftover omelet makes a nice lunch during the week. *serves 6*

In a 12-inch nonstick skillet, heat 2 tablespoons of the oil over medium-high heat. Add the onions and cook until soft, about 5 minutes. Add the potatoes, ½ teaspoon of the salt, and the pepper. Add ⅔ cup water and cover the skillet. Reduce the heat to medium-low and cook until the potatoes are tender, about 15 minutes. Scrape the potato mixture into a large bowl and let cool, stirring occasionally, about 30 minutes. Wipe out and reserve the skillet.

In another large bowl, whisk together the eggs, garlic, olives, thyme, parsley, and remaining ½ teaspoon salt. Fold in the cheese and the cooled potato mixture.

Preheat the broiler.

Add the remaining 2 tablespoons oil to the skillet and heat over medium-high heat. Pour in the egg mixture, spreading evenly. Cook, uncovered, until the sides are set and the top edge begins to brown, about 5 minutes. Run a flexible heat-proof spatula around the sides of the pan to loosen the omelet. Cover tightly, reduce the heat to medium-low, and cook until the center is almost set, about 5 minutes.

Uncover the skillet and broil the omelet until the top is fully cooked and begins to brown, 3 to 4 minutes. Let rest for 2 minutes.

RECIPE CONTINUES

Loosen the omelet again around the sides and underneath as far as possible. Slide the omelet onto a platter and garnish with thyme and parsley sprigs. Cut into 6 wedges and serve each wedge with 2 tablespoons of the romesco sauce.

romesco sauce

This sauce can also be tossed with cooked pasta or rice or served alongside meat or chicken. It will keep, covered in the fridge, for three to four days or can be frozen for up to one month.

MAKES 2 CUPS

1 (15- to 16-ounce) bottle roasted red bell peppers, drained

⅓ cup extra-virgin olive oil

¼ cup tomato paste

¼ cup Marcona almonds or toasted hazelnuts
   (see Cook's Note; page 90)

2 tablespoons sherry wine vinegar

2 garlic cloves, chopped

1 teaspoon smoked paprika

½ teaspoon kosher salt

½ teaspoon freshly ground black pepper

Combine all of the ingredients in a blender or food processor. Blend until the sauce is almost smooth, scraping down the sides of the container occasionally. If the sauce is too thick, blend in 1 teaspoonful water at a time to thin it. Transfer the sauce to a small bowl.

per serving (2 table-spoons): Calories 68; Protein 1g; Carbohydrates 3g; Dietary Fiber 0g; Sugar 1g; Total Fat 6g; Saturated Fat 1g; Sodium 120mg

2 cups unsweetened almond milk or water

1 cup quick-cooking bulgur wheat

½ teaspoon pure vanilla extract

½ teaspoon ground cinnamon

⅛ teaspoon fine sea salt

4 teaspoons extra-virgin olive oil

Poached Mixed Berries (recipe follows)

per serving (includes berries): Calories 277; Protein 6g; Carbohydrates 51g; Dietary Fiber 13g; Sugar 17g; Total Fat 8g; Saturated Fat 1g; Sodium 172mg

per serving: Calories 93; Protein 1g; Carbohydrates 23g; Dietary Fiber 6g; Sugar 17g; Total Fat 1g; Saturated Fat 0g; Sodium 3mg

breakfast bulgur wheat with poached mixed berries

When I can't figure out if I want sweet or savory in the morning, I make this recipe, which is warm and satisfying; the grains have a bit of bite to them, more so than oatmeal. Poaching the berries softens them, sort of turning them into a homemade sugar-free jam. A drizzle of olive oil adds a nice creamy, rich finishing touch. It may sound odd to serve grains with olive oil, but trust me— it works! *serves* 4

In a medium saucepan, combine the almond milk, bulgur wheat, vanilla, cinnamon, and salt. Bring to a boil over medium heat. Lower the heat so that the mixture simmers. Cover the pan and cook until the bulgur is tender, 12 minutes. Spoon into 4 bowls. Drizzle each portion with 1 teaspoon of the olive oil, top with berries, and serve immediately.

poached mixed berries

This recipe works with fresh or frozen berries. If opting for frozen, just make sure the berries are thawed before you start.

SERVES 4

12 large strawberries, hulled and halved, or 1 (10-ounce) bag frozen whole strawberries

1 cup raspberries

1 cup blackberries

1 cup blueberries

¼ cup unsweetened apple juice

1 tablespoon light agave nectar

In a medium saucepan, combine the strawberries, raspberries, blackberries, blueberries, apple juice, and agave. Bring the mixture to a boil over medium-high heat. Lower the heat so that the mixture simmers and cook until the fruit is soft but not mushy, 8 to 10 minutes. Remove the pan from the heat and let cool at least slightly before serving. Stored in a covered container in the refrigerator, leftovers will keep for up to 5 days.

1 cup vanilla-flavored unsweetened almond milk

1 cup plain low-fat (2%) Greek yogurt

2 tablespoons pure maple syrup (preferably grade B), plus 4 teaspoons for serving

1 teaspoon pure vanilla extract

⅛ teaspoon kosher salt

¼ cup chia seeds

1 pint strawberries, hulled and diced

¼ cup sliced almonds, toasted (see Cook's Note)

per serving: Calories 215; Protein 9g; Carbohydrates 27g; Dietary Fiber 8g; Sugar 17g; Total Fat 10g; Saturated Fat 2g; Sodium 112mg

chia seed pudding

This is a real treat: a no-cook creamy pudding that's good for you. Once plumped in almond milk and creamy yogurt, chia seeds remind me of tapioca—only they are high in omega-3s and fiber. Chia seeds can be found in some grocery stores these days as well as in natural foods stores. The great part, too, is that you make this pudding the night before. Come morning, you just pull it out of the fridge and top it with some almonds and fruit, and breakfast is ready. *Serves 4*

In a medium bowl, gently whisk the almond milk, yogurt, the 2 tablespoons maple syrup, vanilla, and salt until just blended. Whisk in the chia seeds. Let stand for 30 minutes. Stir to distribute the seeds if they have settled. Cover and refrigerate overnight.

The next day, in a medium bowl, toss the berries with the remaining 4 teaspoons maple syrup. Mix in the almonds.

Spoon the pudding into 4 bowls or stemmed pudding glasses, mound the berry mixture on top, and serve.

cook's note

To toast sliced almonds, arrange in a single layer on a baking sheet. Bake in a preheated 350°F oven until lightly toasted, 6 to 8 minutes. Let cool completely before using.

lazy sundays

Every Sunday morning Todd cooks breakfast and makes his famous egg scramble surprise; the ingredients vary according to what we have in the refrigerator. Sometimes Jade helps him and sometimes she climbs into bed with me to snuggle.

Then it's mommy-and-me time with Jade; we make popcorn and watch a movie or get our nails done together. Jade always has her favorite Sunday afternoon snack, a chocolate croissant, and then we have family dinner. Todd and I alternate reading to Jade each night. On Sundays, we pick a book with multiple characters and Todd and I act them out with Jade. She especially loves to do this with her princess storybooks! It's the perfect end to family day.

2/3 cup sugar

3 large eggs, at room temperature

Grated zest of 1 medium orange

1/3 cup fresh orange juice, at room temperature

1/4 cup extra-virgin olive oil

3 tablespoons plain low-fat (2%) Greek yogurt, at room temperature

3/4 teaspoon pure vanilla extract

3/4 teaspoon pure almond extract

1 cup all-purpose flour

2/3 cup almond flour

1 1/2 teaspoons baking powder

1/4 teaspoon fine sea salt

1/3 cup sliced almonds, toasted (see Cook's Note, page 29)

per muffin: Calories 200; Protein 5g; Carbohydrates 22g; Dietary Fiber 1g; Sugar 12g; Total Fat 11g; Saturated Fat 1g; Sodium 127mg

orange-scented almond and olive oil muffins

I love to take these muffins to Jade's school for breakfast for her classmates to share. One of the ingredients is almond flour, which I love to use for baking because it adds flavor and protein to replace some of the usual white flour. Almond flour also makes the muffins light and nutty and pairs so well with the sweetness of orange juice and zest. Make a batch of these, freeze them, and then reheat as needed in a low oven. *Makes 12 muffins*

Position an oven rack in the center of the oven and preheat the oven to 325°F. Line 18 muffin cups with paper liners.

Using a hand mixer on medium speed, in a medium bowl, beat the sugar and eggs together until pale and thick, about 2 minutes. Beat in the orange zest and juice, olive oil, yogurt, vanilla, and almond extract.

In a separate bowl, whisk together the all-purpose and almond flours, baking powder, and salt.

In batches, stir the flour mixture into the egg mixture until just blended. Stir in the almonds. Pour heaped 1/3 cupfuls of the batter into the prepared muffin cups. Bake until golden on top and a tester inserted into the center of the muffins comes out with moist crumbs attached, about 20 minutes. Cool in the pan on a wire rack for at least 20 minutes before serving.

½ teaspoon fine sea salt

2 cups old-fashioned rolled oats

Grated zest of ½ lemon, or more to taste

1 teaspoon fresh thyme, or more to taste, chopped

4 teaspoons extra-virgin olive oil

per serving: Calories 190; Protein 5g; Carbohydrates 27g; Dietary Fiber 4g; Sugar 1g; Total Fat 8g; Saturated Fat 1g; Sodium 292mg

oatmeal with olive oil

The person who opened my eyes to eating oatmeal like this is my aunt Raffy. She never understood why we put sugar on it; instead, she has always gone the savory route, flavoring hers with olive oil and salt. After I got over my initial skepticism, I tried it and it was delicious. It has quickly become my go-to for a fast, savory breakfast, even on the road; you can almost always get oatmeal made with hot water and then season it to your liking (I always have packets of olive oil in my purse!). I know it sounds strange but think about it this way: Oats are a carbohydrate just like pasta or rice or mashed potatoes, which you'd eat seasoned with salt and olive oil. But oatmeal, unlike any of those, is a whole grain so it's better for you—and, added bonus, it cooks quickly.

serves 4

In a medium saucepan, bring 3½ cups water and the salt to a boil over medium heat. Add the oats and cook, stirring frequently, until creamy, 6 to 7 minutes (for a thicker consistency, cook for 1 to 2 minutes longer).

Stir in the lemon zest and thyme. Spoon the oatmeal into 4 bowls. Drizzle each portion with 1 teaspoon of the olive oil and serve.

½ teaspoon ground
  cinnamon

2 teaspoons sugar

3½ cups unsweetened
  almond milk or water

1 teaspoon pure vanilla
  extract

⅛ teaspoon fine sea salt

2 cups old-fashioned
  rolled oats

per serving: Calories 195;
Protein 6g; Carbohydrates
31g; Dietary Fiber 5g; Sugar
3g; Total Fat 6g; Saturated
Fat 0g; Sodium 232mg

oatmeal with cinnamon sugar

I'm a big lover of oatmeal in the morning, so I have a few ways to vary it so I don't get bored. I make this recipe with almond milk, which has a nutty flavor that pairs so well with oatmeal and adds protein to your bowl. It also lends a slight creaminess without the need for cream or other dairy. *serves* 4

Combine the cinnamon and sugar in a small bowl.

In a medium saucepan, bring the almond milk, vanilla, and salt to a boil over medium heat. Add the oats and cook, stirring frequently, until creamy, 6 to 7 minutes (for a thicker consistency, cook for 1 to 2 minutes longer).

Spoon the oatmeal into 4 bowls, sprinkle with the cinnamon sugar, and serve.

Vegetable oil cooking spray

2 Granny Smith apples, peeled, cored, and cut into ¾-inch chunks

2 ripe but firm pears, peeled, cored, and cut into ¾-inch chunks

1 pound pineapple pieces

1 pound peach wedges

½ cup unsweetened apple juice

2 tablespoons pure maple syrup

¾ teaspoon ground cinnamon

¼ teaspoon ground allspice

1 cup plus 2 tablespoons low-fat ricotta

per serving: Calories 211; Protein 6g; Carbohydrates 40g; Dietary Fiber 4g; Sugar 30g; Total Fat 4g; Saturated Fat 2g; Sodium 59mg

baked fruit with ricotta

This recipe was inspired by my parents, who used to bake fruit all the time. When we had too much fruit and it was about to go bad before we could eat it all, they'd cut it up, bake it, and then put it in the freezer. My brothers, sister, and I ate it like ice cream. Now I like it warm for breakfast with a dollop of creamy, cold ricotta on top. *serves 6*

Position an oven rack in the center of the oven and preheat the oven to 350°F.

Spray a 9 x 13-inch glass or ceramic baking dish with vegetable oil cooking spray. Add the apples, pears, pineapple, and peaches to the dish. Pour the apple juice and maple syrup over the fruit and sprinkle the cinnamon and allspice evenly over the top. Toss to coat.

Bake for 25 minutes. Stir the fruit and continue to bake until it is soft, about 25 minutes more. Let cool at least slightly before scooping the fruit into bowls and topping each bowl with 3 tablespoons of the ricotta.

my morning routine

At the start of every day, no matter where I am in the world, I make sure I do the same four things:

1 I drink two glasses of warm water with lemon first thing in the morning. You get dehydrated as you sleep and need to help your body rehydrate when you get up. I find warm water less of a shock to my system when I've just woken up.

2 Then I do my yoga. I like to get in thirty minutes to an hour, but if I don't have time for that, I do a bare minimum of three stretch sun salutes—even if I am in a hotel room. Yoga helps me get ready for a new day. It opens up my lungs and gets my blood moving.

3 After yoga I fill the sink with ice water and dunk my face right in. Not only is this incredibly refreshing, but it also works wonders for waking up puffy, sleepy eyes.

4 Finally, I never skip breakfast. Even on the road, in an airport, in a foreign time zone, at the very least I'll eat fruit—preferably a banana, which is filling and doesn't need to be washed—and a hard-boiled egg for protein.

7 to 8 medium strawberries, hulled and thinly sliced

1 tablespoon white wine vinegar

4 large eggs, at room temperature

1 tablespoon heavy cream

2 tablespoons sugar

½ teaspoon kosher salt

3 tablespoons finely chopped fresh mint leaves

1 tablespoon unsalted butter, at room temperature

1½ teaspoons extra-virgin olive oil

per serving: Calories 343; Protein 14g; Carbohydrates 22g; Dietary Fiber 3g; Sugar 17g; Total Fat 22g; Saturated Fat 9g; Sodium 425mg

strawberry-mint omelet

While adults appreciate this slightly sweet twist on an otherwise savory omelet, this was actually one of the first ways I got Jade to eat eggs for breakfast. She's a strawberry girl and will try anything that features her favorite fruit! I like to make a couple of pans of this omelet and serve it for brunch when we are having friends over because it is absolutely beautiful. *Serves 2 or 3*

In a small bowl, toss together the strawberries and vinegar. Allow the mixture to stand for 15 minutes. Strain before using.

In a medium bowl, whisk together the eggs, cream, sugar, and salt until smooth. Stir in the mint.

In a 10-inch nonstick skillet, heat the butter and oil over medium-high heat. Add the egg mixture and cook until almost set, about 4 minutes. Spoon the strawberries in a line across the center of the omelet. Fold the edges of the omelet up over the strawberries. Cook until the egg mixture has set, 3 to 4 minutes.

Cut the omelet into servings and transfer, seam side down, to plates.

5 large kale leaves

2 tablespoons extra-virgin olive oil

1¼ cups grape tomatoes, halved

1 large shallot, chopped

2 garlic cloves, chopped

1 teaspoon chopped fresh thyme

⅛ teaspoon crushed red pepper flakes (optional)

½ teaspoon kosher salt

¼ teaspoon freshly ground black pepper

¼ cup chopped fresh basil leaves

4 large eggs, at room temperature

4 (10-inch) whole-wheat tortillas

¼ cup store-bought plain hummus

per serving: Calories 403; Protein 19g; Carbohydrates 50g; Dietary Fiber 5g; Sugar 4g; Total Fat 17g; Saturated Fat 4g; Sodium 377mg

egg, kale, and tomato breakfast wraps with hummus

When Jade says, "Make me my breakfast sandwich," we know she means this recipe. This is an all-in-one, colorful, hearty wrap that's perfect for making your own. Customize this according to what's in your fridge, swapping spinach for the kale or jarred red bell peppers for the tomatoes. And if you don't have time to poach the eggs, just scramble them instead. *Serves 4*

Cut away and discard the stem from the center of each kale leaf. Coarsely chop the kale into 1-inch pieces. It will look like you have a lot of kale but it will cook down considerably.

Heat the oil in a large nonstick skillet over medium heat. Add the tomatoes, shallot, garlic, thyme, and red pepper flakes, if using. Sauté until the tomatoes and shallot soften, about 4 minutes. Add the kale and sprinkle with the salt and pepper. Toss with 2 wooden spoons until the kale wilts but is still bright green, about 2 minutes. Stir in the basil. Remove from the heat.

Fill a wide saucepan with enough water to measure 2 inches deep. Bring the water to a rolling boil over high heat. Break each egg into a separate tea cup. Turn off the heat under the saucepan. Immediately slide each egg from its cup into a different part of the water (the whites will spread out). Let the eggs stand until the whites are set and the yolks are still very soft to the touch, 3 to 4 minutes.

Meanwhile, using tongs, toast each tortilla directly over high heat until beginning to blacken in spots, about 15 seconds per side. Put the warm tortillas on plates. Spoon 1 tablespoon of hummus on each tortilla and spread to cover, leaving a 1-inch border. Divide the kale mixture over the hummus.

Using a slotted spoon, lift each egg from the water, wiping excess liquid from the bottom of the spoon with paper towels. Put the eggs on top of the kale. Slit the yolks and press on the eggs a bit so the yolks begin to run (this will make them easier to eat). Fold up the bottom of each tortilla and then fold in the sides, leaving the wraps open at the top. Serve.

2 grapefruit

2 oranges

2 tablespoons chopped fresh
   mint leaves

2 cups honey-flavored nonfat
   (0%) Greek yogurt

¼ cup unsalted pumpkin or
   sunflower seeds, toasted
   (see Cook's Note)

per serving: Calories 235;
Protein 13g; Carbohydrates
41g; Dietary Fiber 8g; Sugar
31g; Total Fat 4g; Saturated
Fat 0g; Sodium 28mg

citrus parfaits

Citrus and yogurt make a wonderful pairing, each rounding
the other out. These are filling and refreshing. Pack this in a
container for a great breakfast to go. *serves* 4

Cut off the ends of one of the grapefruits and then use a sharp
knife to slice off all of the peel and the white pith underneath.
Using a paring knife, and holding the grapefruit in your hand,
slice between the membranes to release the segments. Cut the
segments into ½-inch pieces and put into a bowl. Repeat with the
remaining grapefruit and the oranges.

Stir the mint into the citrus in the bowl.

Using a slotted spoon, scoop ¼ cup citrus into the bottom of each
of 4 parfait glasses or bowls. Top each with ¼ cup of the yogurt.
Repeat to make a second layer of citrus and yogurt. Sprinkle the
tops of the parfaits with the pumpkin seeds and serve.

cook's note
To toast pumpkin or sunflower seeds, arrange in a single layer
on a baking sheet. Bake in a preheated 350°F oven until lightly
toasted, 3 to 5 minutes. Let cool completely before using.

salsa

2 medium tomatoes, quartered

¼ packed cup fresh cilantro or flat-leaf parsley leaves

1 garlic clove, crushed

1½ teaspoons extra-virgin olive oil

2 tablespoons fresh lime juice

¼ teaspoon crushed red pepper flakes

½ teaspoon kosher salt

eggs

8 egg whites, at room temperature, or 1 cup pasteurized egg white product, such as Just Whites

½ teaspoon kosher salt

¼ teaspoon freshly ground black pepper

1 tablespoon extra-virgin olive oil

5 scallions, white and green parts, chopped

2 packed cups arugula or baby spinach, coarsely chopped

per serving: Calories 223; Protein 17g; Carbohydrates 15g; Dietary Fiber 4g; Sugar 7g; Total Fat 11g; Saturated Fat 2g; Sodium 527mg

egg white scramble with spicy tomato salsa

This is a clean, fresh dish that is satisfying but keeps me light on my feet. And I can whip it up in no time. I usually have some kind of fresh salsa in my fridge—and, barring that, I *always* have spicy tomato sauce on hand, which makes a great stand-in. I like the spicy kick to the eggs, which adds more flavor and helps me rev up for the day. *serves 2*

for the salsa: Combine the tomatoes, cilantro, garlic, olive oil, lime juice, red pepper flakes, and salt in a food processor. Pulse until the ingredients are combined but still chunky.

for the eggs: In a medium bowl, beat the egg whites, salt, and pepper until frothy.

In a medium nonstick skillet, heat the oil over medium-high heat. Add the scallions and arugula. Cook, stirring occasionally, until the arugula has wilted, about 2 minutes. Add the egg whites and cook, stirring constantly, until the eggs are scrambled and cooked through, 2 to 3 minutes.

Divide the scrambled egg mixture between 2 plates. Top with the salsa and serve.

⅔ cup creamy almond butter

1 tablespoon plus 1 teaspoon honey

1 teaspoon pure vanilla extract

⅛ teaspoon kosher salt

4 slices sprouted whole-grain bread

12 large strawberries, hulled and thinly sliced

4 teaspoons sliced almonds, toasted (see Cook's Note, page 29)

per serving: Calories 387; Protein 10g; Carbohydrates 31g; Dietary Fiber 4g; Sugar 14g; Total Fat 27g; Saturated Fat 3g; Sodium 178mg

almond butter strawberry toast

This tastes as good as it sounds and is my Friday morning breakfast treat. To make it good for me, I go for sprouted bread, which is made from whole grains that have been allowed to sprout before being turned into flour. It is not as processed as the flour in most of the loaves of bread on supermarket shelves and is higher in vitamins. I also opt for all-natural almond butter made with only almonds and oil—no sugar, trans fats, or preservatives. The crowning sweet strawberries seal the deal, though bananas are another favorite. *serves 4*

In a medium bowl, stir together the almond butter, 1 tablespoon of the honey, the vanilla, and salt until well blended.

Toast the bread slices. Spread the almond butter mixture over the pieces of toast. Top with strawberry slices, arranging them close together and pressing down on them slightly so they won't fall off. Drizzle each toast with ¼ teaspoon of the remaining honey. Sprinkle with sliced almonds and serve.

4 tablespoons safflower or grapeseed oil

1½ pounds russet potatoes (about 2 medium), peeled and chopped into 1-inch cubes

1½ teaspoons kosher salt

½ teaspoon freshly ground black pepper

1 medium onion, chopped

1 red bell pepper, cut into ½-inch pieces

4 cups baby spinach leaves

1 tablespoon chopped fresh thyme

½ teaspoon ground nutmeg

Grated zest of ½ medium orange

1 (12-ounce) container extra-firm tofu, drained, patted dry, and cut into ½-inch cubes

per serving: Calories 320; Protein 13g; Carbohydrates 26g; Dietary Fiber 5g; Sugar 3g; Total Fat 20g; Saturated Fat 2g; Sodium 476mg

california tofu hash

This is not your average hash! It's light but has tons of flavor, and I absolutely love it. It's my perfect go-to recipe after a morning of paddle-boarding out in that California sun! *serves* 4

In a 12-inch nonstick skillet, heat 2 tablespoons of the oil over medium-high heat. Add the potatoes, 1 teaspoon of the salt, and ¼ teaspoon of the pepper. Cook, stirring frequently, until brown and crisp, about 25 minutes. Using a slotted spoon, remove the potatoes and drain on paper towels.

To the same pan, add the remaining 2 tablespoons oil, the onion, bell pepper, ¼ teaspoon of the salt, and ⅛ teaspoon of the pepper. Cook, stirring occasionally, over medium-high heat until the vegetables are soft, about 5 minutes. Add the spinach, thyme, nutmeg, orange zest, the remaining ¼ teaspoon salt, and the remaining ⅛ teaspoon pepper. Cook until the spinach is wilted, about 2 minutes.

Add the tofu and cook, stirring, until heated through, about 3 minutes. Stir in the cooked potatoes to warm through, about 1 minute. Serve hot.

juices &

smoothies

juice cleanse

Sometimes after traveling, or when I just don't feel like myself—
whether it's due to inflammation, bloating, or general sluggishness—I turn to
the recipes in this chapter. They help me detox and get back on track, filling me
with essential nutrients that are good for my body. I might have a smoothie for

breakfast, some warm plain brown rice and possibly some scrambled egg whites for lunch, a juice in the afternoon, and then my Detox Broth (page 67) with poached chicken for dinner. I always incorporate some protein when doing a juice cleanse. For me, it's an important component in getting my strength back and feeling balanced.

Some of the recipes in this chapter can be made in a regular blender; some need a high-powered blender, such as a Vitamix, to come together; and others are true juices, requiring an electric juicer. But I've given you options so you can make some of these recipes if you have only a standard blender. If you are in the market for a new blender, consider a Vitamix brand. They are expensive but worth the money; they can liquefy almost anything and froth up fruits and vegetables with the addition of just ice to make smoothie-like treats that are dairy-free and delicious.

I serve the straight juice recipes cold. I know many people recommend drinking them warm or at room temperature but I just can't do it. Chilled, however, they are delicious.

5 ounces baby spinach leaves, rinsed

2 medium carrots, scrubbed

2 apples, halved and cored

2 celery stalks

½ large lemon

1 (2-inch) piece of fresh ginger, peeled

Ice

special equipment: an electric vegetable juicer

rise-and-shine juice

When I'm shooting my show, I like to start my day with this rise-and-shine juice instead of coffee. It gives me energy and nutrients. I drink it over ice as my slightly sweet, refreshing wake-up call. *makes 2¼ cups; serves 2*

Pass the spinach, carrots, apples, celery, lemon, and ginger through a juice maker, according to the manufacturer's directions. Serve over ice.

1½ cups ice

½ cup water

1 medium apple, such as Fuji or Honey Crisp, peeled, cored, and cut into ½-inch pieces

1 celery stalk, coarsely chopped

1 (1-inch) piece of fresh ginger, peeled and coarsely chopped

1 cup packed baby spinach leaves

⅓ cup packed fresh flat-leaf parsley leaves

special equipment: a high-powered blender, such as a Vitamix

per serving: Calories 49; Protein 1g; Carbohydrates 12g; Dietary Fiber 2g; Sugar 8g; Total Fat 0g; Saturated Fat 0g; Sodium 42mg

spinach, ginger, and apple smoothie

If you like a little spice in your smoothie, this is the one for you. I like this as an afternoon pick-me-up; the ginger gives you a jolt of energy. *makes 2 cups; serves 2*

Combine all of the ingredients in the blender and blend on high speed until smooth. Pour into glasses and serve.

3 grapefruits, peeled and halved

2 packed cups of fresh mint

Ice

special equipment: an electric vegetable juicer

per serving: Calories 115; Protein 1g; Carbohydrates 27g; Dietary Fiber 0g; Sugar 27g; Total Fat 0g; Saturated Fat 0g; Sodium 3mg

grapefruit mint juice

I drink this instead of coffee in the afternoon. It's like having grapefruit sorbet after lunch. It clears your palate and wakes it up and readies it for dinner. It's unbelievably refreshing. I always look forward to this one. *makes 2 cups; serves 2*

Pass the grapefruit and mint through a juice maker, according to the manufacturer's directions. Serve over ice.

1½ cups ice

½ cup water

¼ cup plain nonfat (0%) Greek yogurt

1 medium apple, such as Fuji or Honey Crisp, peeled, cored, and chopped

8 medium strawberries, halved

½ medium ripe banana, peeled

1 packed cup baby spinach leaves

per serving: Calories 102; Protein 4g; Carbohydrates 23g; Dietary Fiber 4g; Sugar 17g; Total Fat 1g; Saturated Fat 0g; Sodium 36mg

strawberry and spinach smoothie with yogurt

I make this for Jade because she likes the creaminess. You get just enough from the yogurt here, which makes this taste like a treat. Jade and I share this as an after-school snack. *makes 2 cups; serves 2*

Combine all of the ingredients in the blender and blend on high speed until smooth. Pour into glasses and serve.

1½ cups ice

½ cup coconut water

½ cup unsweetened almond milk

½ medium banana, peeled

3 tablespoons walnut pieces

2 dried dates, coarsely chopped

per serving: Calories 144; Protein 4g; Carbohydrates 17g; Dietary Fiber 3g; Sugar 13g; Total Fat 8g; Saturated Fat 1g; Sodium 109mg

banana, walnut, and date smoothie

When I'm doing a juice cleanse, this can replace a meal for me. It's filling and sweet. Sometimes Todd and I share one for dessert in the summer. *makes 2 cups; serves 2*

Combine all of the ingredients in the blender and blend on high speed until smooth. Pour into glasses and serve.

1 cup ice

6 medium strawberries, hulled and halved

⅓ cup fresh or frozen and thawed blueberries

½ cup packed baby spinach leaves

½ medium ripe banana, peeled

¼ cup store-bought green juice, such as Naked Juice Green Machine

¼ packed cup fresh mint leaves

per serving: Calories 77; Protein 2g; Carbohydrates 19g; Dietary Fiber 3g; Sugar 13g; Total Fat 0g; Saturated Fat 0g; Sodium 20mg

double berry smoothie

This is a classic berry smoothie. Trust me that you don't taste the spinach! The mint is nice and refreshing and the banana helps achieve a creamy texture. *makes 2 cups; serves 2*

Combine all of the ingredients in the blender and blend on high speed until smooth. Pour into glasses and serve.

1 cup ice

½ cup water

1 large apple, such as Fuji
or Honey Crisp, peeled,
cored, and cut into ½-inch
pieces

1 medium cucumber, peeled,
seeded, and cut into
½-inch pieces

4 large kale leaves, center rib
removed

1 celery stalk, coarsely
chopped

special equipment: a
high-powered blender, such
as a Vitamix

per serving: Calories 98;
Protein 2g; Carbohydrates
22g; Dietary Fiber 3g;
Sugar 14g; Fat Total 0g;
Saturated Fat 0g; Sodium
35 mg

kale, apple, and cucumber smoothie

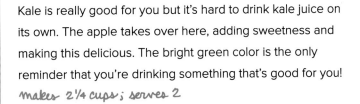

Kale is really good for you but it's hard to drink kale juice on its own. The apple takes over here, adding sweetness and making this delicious. The bright green color is the only reminder that you're drinking something that's good for you!

makes 2¼ cups; serves 2

Combine all of the ingredients in the blender and blend on high speed until smooth. Pour into a tall glass and serve.

yoga

I absolutely love yoga. I do it three or four days a week for thirty minutes to an hour—a mix between flow and hatha. I do it at home, on the beach, in our backyard, or wherever I am. (I take a yoga block and foam roll when I travel.) I always pay special attention to my core (especially post-pregnancy) and upper body. Everyone needs something different.

Morning is the best time for me to do yoga. Sometimes that means it's pretty early—sometimes five a.m. when I am working—but it's worth getting up for. My favorite part is the breathing, which opens up my diaphragm. It gets my body moving, wakes up and strengthens my muscles, and gives me energy for the rest of the day.

1½ cups ice

1½ cups unsweetened almond milk

¼ cup plain nonfat (0%) Greek yogurt

3 dried dates, coarsely chopped

¼ teaspoon pure vanilla extract

⅛ teaspoon fine sea salt

per serving: Calories 83; Protein 4g; Carbohydrates 12g; Dietary Fiber 2g; Sugar 9g; Total Fat 3g; Saturated Fat 0g; Sodium 267mg

vanilla, date, and almond smoothie with yogurt

This sweet and creamy smoothie can also replace a meal if you're on a juice cleanse. Or it can tame a sugar craving if you are in the mood for something a little sweet.

makes 2 cups; serves 2

Combine all of the ingredients in the blender and blend on high speed until smooth. Pour into glasses and serve.

1½ pounds kale

2 medium carrots, scrubbed

2 medium apples, such as Fuji or Honey Crisp, halved and cored

1 small lemon, peeled

special equipment: an electric vegetable juicer

per serving: Calories 109; Protein 2g; Carbohydrates 29g; Dietary Fiber 4g*; Sugar 18g*; Total Fat 0g; Saturated Fat 0g; Sodium 45mg

* Fiber and sugar content may vary slightly depending on juicer used

kale juice

When I need to detox after a lot of travel and changing of time zones, this is my go-to juice. It has just four ingredients. I drink this for breakfast and it reinvigorates me and helps me to get balanced again. *makes 2 cups; serves 2*

Pass all of the ingredients through a juice maker, according to the manufacturer's directions. Pour into glasses and serve.

2 Granny Smith apples, halved and cored

2 medium carrots, scrubbed

1 large red beet, scrubbed and trimmed

1 lemon, peeled

1 (1½-inch) piece of fresh ginger, peeled

½ cup packed fresh flat-leaf parsley leaves

Ice

special equipment: an electric vegetable juicer

per serving: Calories 97; Protein 2g; Carbohydrates 26g; Dietary Fiber 3g*; Sugar 17g*; Total Fat 0g; Saturated Fat 0g; Sodium 64mg

Fiber and sugar content may vary slightly depending on juicer used

beet, ginger, and apple juice

I love the jewel tone of this juice. It's absolutely stunning. You get a nice warmth and spiciness from the ginger and sweetness from the apples. Try this as an afternoon snack instead of hitting the vending machine. *makes 2 cups; serves 2*

Pass the apples, carrots, beet, lemon, ginger, and parsley through a juice maker, according to the manufacturer's directions. Serve over ice.

1 (12-ounce) bone-in, skinless chicken breast half

2 medium carrots, peeled and cut into ½-inch rounds

2 celery stalks, cut into ½-inch pieces

1 (1-inch) piece of fresh ginger, peeled and chopped

3 garlic cloves, peeled

2 shallots, thinly sliced

6 sprigs fresh thyme

8 whole black peppercorns

3 whole cloves

1 dried bay leaf

½ cinnamon stick

per serving (1 cup):
Calories 20*; Protein 3g; Carbohydrates 2g; Dietary Fiber 0g; Sugar 1g; Total Fat 0g*; Saturated Fat 0g; Sodium 0mg

Calories and fat are dependent on the amount of fat removed during preparation and may vary slightly.

detox broth

When I need to detox, this recipe is a lifesaver. It's soothing and warming and I'll sip a cup of it in the morning, another at lunch, and the last one in the afternoon. I make the broth, cool it, and freeze it in ice trays to portion. If I've been out at breakfast and lunch, it can even be a light dinner; I'll heat up a handful of cubes with a little of the poached chicken and add some vegetables, such as sliced carrots, celery, baby spinach, or peas.

makes 3½ cups broth; serves 3

In a medium saucepan, bring 6 cups water, the chicken, carrots, celery, ginger, garlic, shallots, thyme, peppercorns, cloves, bay leaf, and cinnamon stick to a boil over medium-high heat. Reduce the heat and simmer for 1 hour. Strain the liquid, reserving the chicken and vegetables for another use.

Cool the broth and refrigerate for up to 2 days or strain and freeze for up to 1 month.

FRITTATA with Tuna and Tomatoes

KALE AND MUSHROOM WRAP

NONNA'S ARTICHOKES

SWEET POTATOES with Creamy Tofu-Lime Vinaigrette

CHICKEN CHOPPED SALAD in Butter Lettuce Cups

UPDATED WALDORF SALAD with Apple Vinaigrette

CURRIED CHICKEN AND APPLE WRAPS

CHICKEN SALAD with Roasted Root Vegetable Vinaigrette

LEMON-MUSTARD POTATO SALAD

BUTTER LETTUCE AND TUNA SALAD with Pear Dressing

FARFALLE with Chicken, Cremini Mushrooms, and Swiss Chard

STUFFED BELL PEPPERS

WHOLE-WHEAT ORZO with Artichoke Pesto

TURKEY, KALE, AND BROWN RICE SOUP

GREEN PEA, LETTUCE, AND FENNEL SOUP

ROASTED TOMATO SOUP with Halibut

ARTICHOKE SOUP with Fresh Mint

lunch

QUINOA, ROASTED EGGPLANT,
AND APPLE SALAD
with Cumin Vinaigrette

CHICKEN AND HONEY-
MUSTARD PINWHEELS

SHRIMP AND AVOCADO
SALAD

PITA AND GRILLED
VEGETABLE PANZANELLA

RADICCHIO, PEAR,
AND ARUGULA SALAD

QUINOA PILAF

BROWN AND WILD RICE
with Brussels Sprouts

HERBED QUINOA

BEET AND MARINATED GOAT
CHEESE SALAD

WHEAT BERRIES
with Strawberries

CHICKEN, MANGO, AND
BLACK BEANS WITH
LIME-ALMOND DRESSING

FENNEL, RADISH,
AND CHIVE SALAD

QUINOA with
Black Beans and Hominy

WHOLE-WHEAT PEARL
COUSCOUS SALAD
with Smoked Paprika

HALIBUT CEVICHE SALAD
with Avocado Salsa

SOBA NOODLE SALAD

GREEK TABBOULEH SALAD
with Kale

6 large eggs, at room temperature

¼ cup whole milk, at room temperature

3 tablespoons chopped fresh flat-leaf parsley leaves

1 tablespoon anchovy paste

½ teaspoon kosher salt

½ teaspoon freshly ground black pepper

2 (5-ounce) cans tuna packed in olive oil, such as Flott, drained and flaked into ½-inch pieces

1 tablespoon extra-virgin olive oil

1 tablespoon unsalted butter, at room temperature

2 plum tomatoes, seeded and chopped

per serving: Calories 297; Protein 25g; Carbohydrates 3g; Dietary Fiber 1g; Sugar 3g; Total Fat 19g; Saturated Fat 6g; Sodium 695mg

frittata with tuna and tomatoes

When I was growing up, we used to have frittata for dinner often because it is fast and easy to make, and we'd snack on leftovers after coming home from school the next day. It's good anytime, really, and makes a great make-ahead lunch to take to work, either with a small green salad or sandwiched between two slices of bread. Canned tuna adds needed flavor and olive oil makes it rich and smooth; both add a meaty savoriness to the frittata. *serves* 4

Position an oven rack in the center of the oven and preheat the oven to 400°F.

In a large bowl, whisk together the eggs, milk, parsley, anchovy paste, salt, and pepper. Fold in the tuna.

In an ovenproof, 10-inch nonstick skillet, heat the oil and butter over medium-high heat. Add the egg mixture and cook, without stirring, for 5 minutes. Scatter the tomatoes on top and continue to cook until a crust forms on the underside and the sides of the mixture have set, about 3 minutes longer.

Put the skillet in the oven and bake until the center is set, 6 to 8 minutes. Using a heat-resistant spatula, loosen the sides of the frittata and slide onto a serving plate.

Cut the frittata into wedges and serve hot or at room temperature. The frittata will keep for 3 to 4 days in a covered container in the refrigerator.

3 tablespoons olive oil

1 large or 2 small shallots, thinly sliced

1 medium leek, white and pale green part only, rinsed and thinly sliced

8 ounces mushrooms, such as cremini, button, or stemmed shiitake, sliced (4 cups)

½ teaspoon kosher salt

½ teaspoon freshly ground black pepper

1 (8-ounce) bunch kale, stemmed and coarsely chopped

¼ cup vegetable broth

⅓ cup unsweetened dried cranberries

2 ounces goat cheese, crumbled (¼ cup), at room temperature

4 (10-inch) high-fiber multigrain wraps

per serving: Calories 392; Protein 18g; Carbohydrates 51g; Dietary Fiber 17g; Sugar 3g; Total Fat 20g; Saturated Fat 6g; Sodium 535mg

kale and mushroom wrap

I love vegetables but some days I just can't eat another salad for lunch! Here is a great way to get your veggies and make them interesting. When you throw warm kale and mushrooms into a wrap with a little goat cheese, they melt the cheese a bit. Cranberries add a little unexpected chewy sweetness. This is easy to pack for lunch on the go. *Serves 4*

In a large skillet, heat the oil over medium-high heat. Add the shallot, leek, mushrooms, salt, and pepper. Cook, stirring frequently, until the vegetables are soft, about 8 minutes. Add the kale and cook until wilted, about 8 minutes. Add the broth and cranberries. Bring to a boil and scrape up the brown bits that cling to the bottom of the pan with a wooden spoon.

Remove the pan from the heat and stir in the goat cheese. Divide the filling among the wraps. Fold the bottom of each wrap up and roll in the sides, like a burrito, and cut in half. Serve hot.

Vegetable oil cooking spray

3 medium artichokes

1 large lemon, halved

4 tablespoons extra-virgin olive oil

3 garlic cloves, peeled

3 tablespoons anchovy paste

¼ teaspoon kosher salt

¼ teaspoon freshly ground black pepper

4 ounces mushrooms, such as cremini, button, or stemmed shiitake, sliced (2 cups)

3 tomatoes, cored and chopped

½ cup medium black olives, pitted and coarsely chopped

1 tablespoon capers, drained and rinsed

2 tablespoons freshly grated Parmesan cheese

2 tablespoons plain dry bread crumbs

per serving: Calories 184; Protein 5g; Carbohydrates 15g; Dietary Fiber 5g; Sugar 4g; Total Fat 12g; Saturated Fat 2g; Sodium 530mg

nonna's artichokes

Artichokes are often served like this as a light lunch in Italy, especially if you know you're going out that night for a big meal. My grandmother was a huge lover of artichokes and stuffed them many different ways; for us kids, she would use leftover risotto and serve them to us at lunchtime. I like to make these on the weekend, stuffing them with mushrooms, tomatoes, olives, capers, and Parmesan. No matter the filling, artichokes always remind me of my grandmother. *serves 6*

Spray a 9 x 13-inch glass baking dish with vegetable oil spray.

Bring a large stockpot of salted water to a boil over high heat.

Cut the tops off of the artichokes and trim the stems. Halve the artichokes lengthwise and rub the cut sides of the artichokes with the lemon halves. Squeeze the juice from the lemon halves into the water and add the lemon halves, too. Add the artichoke halves, cover, and cook until just tender, 20 minutes. Drain in a colander, stem side up, to allow any excess water to drain from the leaves. When the artichokes are cool enough to handle, use a small spoon to scoop out and discard the fuzzy chokes.

In a large nonstick skillet, heat 3 tablespoons of the oil over medium heat. Add the garlic and cook until golden brown, 2 to 3 minutes. Remove the garlic and discard. Remove the pan from the heat and let the oil cool slightly. Whisk in the anchovy paste until smooth.

Return the pan with the anchovy oil to the heat and put the artichokes, cut side down, in the pan. Cook for 6 minutes. Turn the artichokes over and cook until tender, another 6 minutes. Put the artichokes, cut side up, in the prepared baking dish and season with the salt and pepper. Reserve the pan juices.

Preheat the broiler.

Return the pan to the heat and add the mushrooms, tomatoes, olives, and capers. Cook, stirring frequently, until the mushrooms are soft, about 7 minutes. Spoon the mushroom mixture into the artichokes, about ⅓ cup in each artichoke.

In a small bowl, mix together the cheese and bread crumbs and sprinkle 1 teaspoon over each artichoke. Drizzle with the remaining 1 tablespoon of olive oil.

Broil the artichokes until golden brown, 2 to 3 minutes. Serve hot.

I was taught at a very young age, by my mom and grandma
Nonna, always to take care of my skin. When I started wearing makeup as a
teenager, I learned to always make sure to remove it all at the end of the day. It
sounds simple, but is the most important thing to remember at the end of a long

day. My nighttime beauty
routine is one that has been
learned and passed down for
generations: Floss and brush
teeth, remove makeup and
exfoliate face, and apply face
cream and eye cream. Another
part of my ritual is a warm cup
of chamomile and mint tea
after dinner to clean off the
day and get ready for the next,
a fresh start!

My skin tends to get dry, due
to frequent travel and good
old-fashioned genetics, so
I prefer water-based facial
products. I try to avoid anything
with alcohol in it as it tends
to be a little harsh on already

dehydrated skin. Instead, I look for plumping, collagen-based creams for my face. Another very important ingredient for happy skin is sunscreen. Can't say it enough! I always wear at least 30 SPF on my face, neck, and décolletage. I exfoliate those same areas nightly with a homemade paste of three tablespoons white rice flour mixed with two tablespoons olive oil (almond or grapeseed oil will work just as well, too). I apply it with a soft makeup brush, let it sit for five minutes, and then gently scrub in a circular motion with my fingertips. I rinse with warm water but always follow with a cold splash to seal up the pores. If you have oily skin, you can substitute water or, even better, aloe gel for the oil, changing the ratio to one part flour and two parts liquid. For a more masklike consistency, add an extra tablespoon of rice flour to the mixture. I always apply my face and eye lotions after the scrub. Todd thinks I am nuts for all my little lotion bottles, but my skin loves it! I try to get a proper facial every six weeks to help clean away the old layers of skin and keep the new skin fresh.

Once every three months, my aunt Raffy, my sister, and I all head to the same Korean spa for a head-to-toe scrub, a tradition my aunt started. It is an inexpensive indulgence that we look forward to as much for the time we get to spend together as for the actual pampering. We get scrubbed, then rubbed (complete with oils to condition our hair and scalps), and have facials with fresh cucumbers. It's a combination of the treatments and the girl time, but by the time we are finished, we are utterly rejuvenated, as if every toxin has left our bodies, and our skin positively glows.

Vegetable oil cooking spray

2½ pounds sweet potatoes or red garnet yams (about 3 large), peeled and cut into ¾-inch pieces

2 tablespoons extra-virgin olive oil

1 teaspoon kosher salt

Creamy Tofu-Lime Vinaigrette (recipe follows)

1 Granny Smith apple, cored and cut into ½-inch pieces

⅓ cup unsweetened dried cranberries

¼ cup pumpkin seeds, toasted (see Cook's Note, page 46)

per serving (includes vinaigrette): Calories 318; Protein 6g; Carbohydrates 56g; Dietary Fiber 7g; Sugar 26g; Total Fat 9g; Saturated Fat 1g; Sodium 520mg

sweet potatoes with creamy tofu-lime vinaigrette

I am a big lover of sweet potatoes. Why? Because they're *sweet*! But, they're also good for you. Tofu adds a little protein to this recipe. Instead of adding it directly to the sweet potatoes, I use it to make a creamy but tangy vinaigrette. *serves* 4

Position an oven rack in the center of the oven and preheat the oven to 375°F.

Spray a rimmed baking sheet with vegetable oil cooking spray. Toss the sweet potatoes, olive oil, and salt on the baking sheet. Roast until golden and tender, 35 to 40 minutes. Transfer to a large bowl.

Pour the vinaigrette over the potatoes. Add the apple, cranberries, and pumpkin seeds. Toss until all the ingredients are coated. Refrigerate for at least 1 hour before serving.

creamy tofu-lime vinaigrette

MAKES ABOUT ¾ CUP

½ cup (4 ounces) silken tofu

3 tablespoons fresh lime juice (about 3 large limes)

1 tablespoon pure maple syrup

¾ teaspoon kosher salt

¼ teaspoon freshly ground black pepper

In a blender, combine all of the ingredients and process until smooth. The vinaigrette will keep covered in the refrigerator for up to 2 days.

dressing

2 tablespoons apple cider vinegar

1 tablespoon fresh lemon juice

1 garlic clove, minced

¼ teaspoon kosher salt

⅛ teaspoon freshly ground black pepper

⅓ cup extra-virgin olive oil

salad

1 cup (¼-inch) diced cooked skinless chicken breast

1 cup coarsely chopped baby arugula

½ avocado, finely diced

¼ fennel bulb, chopped into ¼-inch pieces

½ cup diced feta cheese

⅓ cup thinly sliced sun-dried tomatoes

8 kalamata olives, pitted and chopped

¼ teaspoon kosher salt

⅛ teaspoon freshly ground black pepper

12 butter lettuce leaves

per serving: Calories 237; Protein 10g; Carbohydrates 6g; Dietary Fiber 2g; Sugar 2g; Total Fat 20g; Saturated Fat 4g; Sodium 371mg

chicken chopped salad in butter lettuce cups

I love chopped salads; you get so many great tastes in one bite. This recipe is my twist on a traditional chicken chopped salad. Instead of mixing in the lettuce, I use it as a wrap for the salad, which—like every good chopped salad—is studded with so many yummy flavors: chunks of chicken, creamy avocado, salty feta, crunchy fennel, peppery arugula, and bits of sun-dried tomatoes and briny olives. If packing this up to go, keep the salad and lettuce separate so the lettuce leaves don't wilt. *serves 6*

for the dressing: In a small bowl, combine the vinegar, lemon juice, garlic, salt, and pepper. Gradually add the oil, whisking until the dressing is thick.

for the salad: In a large bowl, combine the chicken, arugula, avocado, fennel, feta, sun-dried tomatoes, olives, salt, and pepper. Add the dressing to the salad and toss to coat.

Fill the lettuce leaves with the salad. Arrange the lettuce leaves on a platter and serve.

couscous

1 tablespoon safflower or grapeseed oil

½ cup whole-wheat pearl couscous

¼ teaspoon kosher salt

vinaigrette

¼ cup apple cider vinegar

1 tablespoon honey

1½ teaspoons kosher salt

¼ teaspoon freshly ground black pepper

⅓ cup safflower or grapeseed oil

salad

1 large Gala apple, cored and cut into ¼- to ½-inch dice

1 small fennel bulb, chopped into ¼- to ½-inch pieces

1 cup small green seedless grapes, halved

¾ cup walnut pieces, toasted (see Cook's Note, page 89)

6 large outer leaves from a large radicchio

per serving: Calories 360; Protein 6g; Carbohydrates 33g; Dietary Fiber 6g; Sugar 12g; Total Fat 25g; Saturated Fat 2g; Sodium 352mg

updated waldorf salad with apple vinaigrette

My mother-in-law first introduced me to Waldorf salad a long time ago. What I love in a Waldorf are the crunchy grapes, apples, and nuts; and I always thought I'd prefer the salad without the mayonnaise. So I kept the parts I like and turned the dish into something lighter by adding whole-wheat pearl couscous and substituting an apple cider vinaigrette for the mayo dressing. *serves 6*

for the couscous: In a small saucepan, heat the oil over medium-high heat. Add the couscous and toast until the couscous is lightly golden, about 4 minutes. Add ¾ cup water and the salt and bring to a boil. Lower the heat so that the water simmers, cover the pan, and cook until the liquid is absorbed, about 10 minutes. Uncover the pan and set aside to cool.

for the vinaigrette: In a small bowl, whisk together the vinegar, honey, salt, pepper, and oil.

for the salad: In a large bowl, toss together the apple, fennel, grapes, walnuts, and couscous. Drizzle the vinaigrette over the salad, tossing until coated.

Put 1 radicchio leaf on each plate. Spoon the salad into each leaf, allowing some to spill over.

dressing

¼ cup mango chutney

¼ cup plain low-fat (2%) Greek yogurt

1½ teaspoons curry powder

1 teaspoon extra-virgin olive oil

2 teaspoons fresh lime juice (about 1 large lime)

½ teaspoon kosher salt

¼ teaspoon freshly ground black pepper

salad

¾ cup (¼-inch) diced cooked skinless chicken breast

¾ cup canned chickpeas, rinsed, drained, and coarsely chopped

½ small head romaine lettuce, thinly sliced (about 2 cups)

1 Gala apple, cut into ¼-inch pieces

2 ounces fresh goat cheese, crumbled (¼ cup)

½ cup chopped scallions, white and green parts

½ cup chopped fresh mint leaves

2 tablespoons raisins

⅛ teaspoon hot sauce (optional)

4 (10-inch) high-fiber multigrain wraps

per serving: Calories 353; Protein 26g; Carbohydrates 47g; Dietary Fiber 17g; Sugar 17g; Total Fat 12g; Saturated Fat 5g; Sodium 598mg

curried chicken and apple wraps

This recipe makes a slightly spicy, boldly flavored, creamy salad by substituting Greek yogurt for the mayonnaise that overpowers so many curried chicken salads. Here the sweet-tart mango chutney and fresh mint really shine. In case you hadn't noticed by now, I am a big fan of using whole-wheat wraps instead of bread. They satisfy my carb cravings without overdoing it.
serves 4

for the dressing: In a large bowl, whisk together the chutney, yogurt, curry powder, oil, lime juice, salt, and pepper.

for the salad: Add to the dressing the chicken, chickpeas, lettuce, apple, goat cheese, scallions, mint, raisins, and hot sauce, if using.

Spoon the filling into the center of each wrap, leaving a 2- to 3-inch border. Fold the bottom flap of the wrap up and over the filling. Fold in the sides and roll up tightly to enclose the filling. Cut each wrap in half and serve.

acupuncture

After I had Jade, I started getting sinus infections frequently and I wanted to find ways to treat and prevent them instead of just taking antibiotics. My yoga instructor suggested I see an acupuncturist. I was skeptical but figured I had nothing to lose. And I have to say that while I started it to help with my sinuses, acupuncture has had so many more benefits for me.

When I get acupuncture, I have no choice but to turn off my brain. I literally fall asleep! I've never found anything else that helps me meditate and tune out the way acupuncture does. I also think it rejuvenates the skin on my face. It helps cells to heal and reproduce—naturally, instead of through injections and other things some women turn to in their forties.

Roughly twice a year, I go once a week for ten to twelve weeks at a time. You do have to get over the needles, which are, I admit, a bit odd to see at first. But they don't hurt. I've even converted my sister and some friends.

1 head romaine lettuce, chopped

1 head radicchio, chopped

1 Belgian endive, chopped

2 cups (½-inch) diced cooked skinless chicken breast

½ cup Roasted Root Vegetable Vinaigrette (recipe follows)

per serving (includes vinaigrette): Calories 163; Protein 17g; Carbohydrates 11g; Dietary Fiber 4g; Sugar 3g; Total Fat 6g; Saturated Fat 1g; Sodium 101mg

per serving (2 tablespoons): Calories 72; Protein 1g; Carbohydrates 6g; Dietary Fiber 1g; Sugar 3g; Total Fat 5g; Saturated Fat 1g; Sodium 53mg

chicken salad with roasted root vegetable vinaigrette

This is a great way to use up leftover roasted vegetables and chicken and turn them into a light salad. The roasted veggies are more interesting the second time around in a vinaigrette as opposed to just on their own. Even when I don't have leftover roasted veggies, I have been known to toss some raw ones in the oven just to make this delicious dressing, which I eat on everything: pasta, grilled fish, and, obviously, chicken. The chicken for this salad can be warm or cold, straight from the fridge. *serves 6*

In a large bowl, combine the lettuce, radicchio, endive, and chicken. Add the vinaigrette and toss to coat.

roasted root vegetable vinaigrette

MAKES ABOUT 2½ CUPS

2 medium carrots, peeled and cut into 1-inch pieces

2 medium parsnips, peeled and cut into 1-inch pieces

1 large shallot, quartered

⅓ cup plus 2 tablespoons extra-virgin olive oil

1⅓ cups low-sodium chicken broth

¼ cup frozen unsweetened apple juice concentrate, thawed

3 tablespoons apple cider vinegar

1 teaspoon pure maple syrup

¾ teaspoon kosher salt

¼ teaspoon freshly ground black pepper

Preheat the oven to 425°F.

On a rimmed baking sheet, toss the carrots, parsnips, and shallot with 2 tablespoons of the olive oil. Roast until the vegetables are tender, about 30 minutes. Set aside to cool.

Combine the carrots, parsnips, shallot, remaining ⅓ cup oil, the chicken broth, apple juice concentrate, vinegar, maple syrup, salt, and pepper in a blender or food processor. Blend until smooth.

dressing

2 tablespoons Dijon mustard

1 tablespoon chopped fresh thyme leaves

Grated zest of 1 large lemon

3 tablespoons fresh lemon juice (from 1 large lemon)

3 tablespoons extra-virgin olive oil

½ teaspoon kosher salt

¼ teaspoon freshly ground black pepper

salad

1½ pounds baby red-skinned potatoes, halved

½ teaspoon kosher salt

¼ teaspoon freshly ground black pepper

1 yellow or red bell pepper, cut into thin strips

4 cups arugula (about 4 ounces)

¼ cup walnut pieces or sliced almonds, toasted (see Cook's Note)

per serving: Calories 290; Protein 6g; Carbohydrates 32g; Dietary Fiber 5g; Sugar 3g; Total Fat 16g; Saturated Fat 2g; Sodium 477mg

lemon-mustard potato salad

This hearty, colorful vegetarian lunch totally satisfies because it has tons of flavor from nuts, Dijon mustard, lemon zest and juice, and fresh thyme. It's truly a potato *salad*—with plenty of arugula and bits of chopped bell pepper. This dish keeps well and can even be served as a side at dinner. Because it can sit well on a buffet table, it goes with everything, and everyone can eat it (it's actually vegan), this is my potluck lunch go-to recipe. *serves 4*

Position an oven rack in the center of the oven and preheat the oven to 375°F. Line a heavy rimmed baking sheet with parchment paper.

for the dressing: In a large bowl, whisk together the mustard, thyme, lemon zest, lemon juice, olive oil, salt, and pepper until smooth. Remove 3 tablespoons of the dressing and reserve.

for the salad: Add the potatoes to the bowl and toss until coated with dressing. Arrange the potatoes in an even layer on the prepared baking sheet. Season with the salt and pepper. Roast until golden and tender, about 40 minutes.

In a large bowl, toss together the reserved 3 tablespoons dressing, the bell pepper, and the arugula. Arrange on a platter. Spoon the roasted potatoes on top and sprinkle with the nuts.

cook's note

To toast the walnuts, arrange in a single layer on a baking sheet. Bake in a preheated 350°F oven until lightly toasted, 6 to 8 minutes. Cool completely before using.

butter lettuce and tuna salad with pear dressing

This is my take on a wedge salad like one you'd find as a side in a steak restaurant—a salad that often seems heavier than the steak itself! I replaced some of the ingredients with ones that are still tasty but you can feel good about eating, and I turned it into a chopped salad. But it still reminds me of a steakhouse salad! It's meaty from the tuna, avocados and hazelnuts add richness to replace the usual gobs of cheese, and diced pear adds sweetness along with a light fresh pear dressing. Yum. *serves* 4

for the dressing: In a blender, blend together the diced pear, oil, pear nectar, vinegar, lemon juice, mustard, salt, and pepper until smooth.

for the salad: Put the lettuce, pear, avocado, hazelnuts, and tuna in a bowl. Toss with the dressing and serve.

cook's note

To toast hazelnuts, arrange in a single layer on a baking sheet. Bake in a preheated 350°F oven until lightly toasted, 8 to 10 minutes. Let cool completely before using.

makeup basics

Even if i am rushing out of the house with my hair up in a clip, I always wear some kind of tinted moisturizer or light foundation (with SPF 30) to even out my skin and some concealer under my eyes. (Between being a mom, working, and traveling, I don't often get to catch up on my beauty rest!) A bit of blush works wonders for perking up cheeks and I think a quick brush of black mascara (preferably thickening, as opposed to lengthening) and a shimmery colored lip gloss are a bare minimum for me. If I have a bit more time, I like a little bronzer on the top of my face and on my neck.

When I am working or going out, I often go for a full-on smoky eye with liner and shadow. In that case, I stick with lip gloss. If I have on only mascara—no liner or shadow—I opt for a lipstick to get a little more color on my lips. But to tell you the truth, I prefer lip gloss; it's so much more moisturizing than lipstick.

EYELINER

BLUSH BRUSH

SHIMMERY
LIP GLOSS

Koh Gen Do°
MAIFANSHI
Lip Gloss

BRONZER

PERFUME

LIPSTICK
PENCIL

- 3 tablespoons extra-virgin olive oil
- 1 large or 2 small shallots, sliced
- 1 pound cremini mushrooms, sliced
- ¼ cup dry white wine
- 2 teaspoons chopped fresh thyme
- 1½ teaspoons kosher salt
- ¾ teaspoon freshly ground black pepper
- 1¼ cups low-sodium chicken broth
- 1 (12-ounce) bunch of Swiss chard, center stems removed, leaves chopped into 1-inch pieces
- ⅓ cup mascarpone cheese, at room temperature
- 1 pound farfalle pasta
- 2 cups (½-inch) diced cooked skinless chicken breast

per serving: Calories 515; Protein 30g; Carbohydrates 64g; Dietary Fiber 4g; Sugar 6g; Total Fat 16g; Saturated Fat 5g; Sodium 460mg

farfalle with chicken, cremini mushrooms, and swiss chard

It's no secret that I love pasta. But lately I've been eating it more at lunch instead of at dinner. That way I have the whole afternoon to use the energy. In the fall and winter months, I crave this hearty pasta salad. I like it warm but it is also good at room temperature; I make it the day before and then pack some up for Todd to take to work. *serves 6*

In a large sauté pan, heat the oil over medium-high heat. Add the shallots and mushrooms and cook until tender, 10 to 12 minutes. Add the wine, thyme, ½ teaspoon of the salt, and ¼ teaspoon of the pepper. Simmer until the wine has mostly evaporated, about 3 minutes.

Pour in the broth and bring to a simmer. In batches, add the chard and cook until wilted, about 7 minutes. Season with the remaining 1 teaspoon salt and ½ teaspoon pepper. Remove the pan from the heat and stir in the mascarpone.

Bring a large pot of salted water to a boil over high heat. Add the pasta and cook, stirring occasionally, until tender but still firm to the bite, 8 to 10 minutes. Drain, reserving about 1 cup of the pasta water. Transfer the pasta to a large bowl.

Add the mushroom sauce and chicken to the pasta. Toss until all of the ingredients are coated and then serve.

peppers

Vegetable oil cooking spray

3 medium red bell peppers, halved lengthwise, cored, and seeded

1 tablespoon extra-virgin olive oil

filling

Vegetable oil cooking spray

2 (8-ounce) Japanese eggplants, trimmed and cut into ⅓-inch pieces

1 tablespoon extra-virgin olive oil

½ teaspoon kosher salt

½ (26-ounce) jar tomato-basil sauce

4 ounces firm tofu, drained, patted dry, and cut into ⅓-inch pieces

¼ cup medium black olives, chopped

½ cup medium green olives, chopped

1 tablespoon rinsed and drained capers

½ teaspoon freshly ground black pepper

topping

¼ cup sliced almonds

2 tablespoons freshly grated Parmesan cheese

2 tablespoons extra-virgin olive oil

per serving: Calories 224; Protein 5g; Carbohydrates 17g; Dietary Fiber 7g; Sugar 7g; Total Fat 6g; Saturated Fat 2g; Sodium 472mg

stuffed bell peppers

These vegetarian stuffed peppers are nice hot on the weekends for lunch at home and at room temp as leftovers for a quick weekday lunch. The filling is a cross between a Sicilian pasta sauce and ratatouille, with a bit more texture than both. I roast the eggplant before combining it with tofu, tomato sauce, olives, and capers. *Serves 6*

Position an oven rack in the center of the oven and preheat the oven to 400°F.

for the peppers: Spray a small baking dish or baking sheet with vegetable oil cooking spray. Arrange the peppers, cut side up, on the baking sheet and drizzle with the olive oil. Bake until the peppers are tender but still holding their shape, 30 to 35 minutes.

for the filling: Spray a 9-inch pie dish with vegetable oil cooking spray. Add the eggplant pieces and toss with the olive oil and salt. Roast next to the peppers until tender and golden, about 30 minutes.

In a medium saucepan, combine the tomato sauce, tofu, olives, capers, and pepper. Bring to a simmer and cook until slightly thickened, about 15 minutes. Stir in the eggplant.

for the topping: In a food processor, blend the almonds and cheese until finely ground.

Preheat the broiler.

Spoon the filling into the bell peppers and sprinkle each pepper with 1 tablespoon of the topping. Drizzle with the olive oil. Broil until a golden crust forms, 2 to 3 minutes.

1 pound whole-wheat orzo
    pasta

2 ears corn, shucked and
    silks removed

pesto

1 (12-ounce) package frozen
    artichoke hearts, thawed

¼ cup walnut pieces, toasted
    (see Cook's Note, page 89)

½ cup fresh flat-leaf parsley
    leaves

½ cup fresh oregano leaves

Grated zest of 1 large lemon

¼ cup fresh lemon juice (from
    1 large lemon)

1 garlic clove, smashed

½ teaspoon kosher salt

½ teaspoon freshly ground
    black pepper

¾ cup extra-virgin olive oil

2 cups cherry tomatoes,
    halved

1½ cups freshly grated
    Parmesan cheese

per serving: Calories 704;
Protein 22g; Carbohydrates
68g; Dietary Fiber 8g;
Sugar 5g; Total Fat 9g;
Saturated Fat 8g; Sodium
505mg

whole-wheat orzo
with artichoke pesto

Once you make this pasta and taste it, you are going to start craving it all the time! The grilled corn adds a nice smoky flavor while the artichoke pesto lends richness to the dish. The cheese-free (vegan) pesto gets its flavor from a combo of fresh oregano and parsley, walnuts, artichokes, and lemon. I could eat it by the spoonful, it's so good! You can dress this up with shrimp or salmon, but I like it just the way it is. *serves 6*

Bring a large pot of salted water to a boil over high heat. Add the pasta and cook, stirring occasionally, until tender but still firm to the bite, about 8 minutes. Drain, reserving ½ cup pasta water, and put the pasta in a large bowl.

Put a grill pan over medium-high heat or preheat a gas or charcoal grill.

Grill the corn, turning frequently, until the corn is tender, about 10 minutes. Allow the corn to cool slightly. Using a large knife, remove the kernels from the cob and add the kernels to the bowl.

for the pesto: In a food processor, combine 2 cups of the artichokes, the walnuts, parsley, oregano, lemon zest, lemon juice, garlic, salt, pepper, and oil. Blend, scraping down the sides of the bowl as needed, until the mixture is thick and smooth.

Chop the remaining artichoke hearts into ¾-inch pieces and add to the bowl. Add the pesto, tomatoes, cheese, and reserved pasta water. Toss until all the ingredients are coated. Serve warm or at room temperature.

- 2 tablespoons extra-virgin olive oil
- 5 large shallots, chopped
- 3 medium carrots, peeled and cut into ½-inch pieces
- 1 large red bell pepper, cut into ½-inch pieces
- 8 ounces ground white turkey meat, broken into small chunks
- 1 tablespoon herbes de Provence
- 5 cups low-sodium chicken broth
- 1 (15-ounce) can diced tomatoes, drained
- 1 cup cooked brown rice
- 1 small bunch kale, center ribs removed, leaves coarsely chopped (4 packed cups)
- 1 teaspoon kosher salt
- ½ teaspoon freshly ground black pepper
- ¼ cup chopped fresh flat-leaf parsley leaves
- ¼ cup freshly grated Parmesan cheese

per serving: Calories 361; Protein 24g; Carbohydrates 39g; Dietary Fiber 6g; Sugar 10g; Total Fat 12g; Saturated Fat 3g; Sodium 627mg

turkey, kale, and brown rice soup

I *live* on this hearty delicious soup in winter! I start making it right after Thanksgiving using leftover turkey. I absolutely love it; it just makes me happy and is one of those dishes I crave when it is cool outside. Also, it's really pretty, which soups aren't always.

serves 4

Heat the oil in a large pot over medium-high heat. Add the shallots, carrots, and bell pepper and sauté, stirring frequently, until beginning to brown and soften slightly, 8 to 10 minutes. Add the turkey and stir until the meat turns white and begins to color very slightly around the edges, 5 to 7 minutes. Add the herbes de Provence and stir for 1 minute.

Add the broth, diced tomatoes, and cooked rice and bring to a boil. Stir in the kale and season with ¾ teaspoon of the salt and the black pepper. Reduce the heat to medium-low. Cover and simmer until the vegetables are tender, about 15 minutes. Season with the remaining ¼ teaspoon salt.

Ladle the soup into bowls. Sprinkle with the parsley and the Parmesan cheese.

3 tablespoons unsalted
butter

1 medium fennel bulb,
chopped (about 2 cups),
fronds reserved for garnish

2 large shallots, chopped

1 medium head Bibb lettuce,
cut into ½-inch-wide strips
(4 cups lightly packed)

1 (10-ounce) package frozen
petite peas

1½ cups low-sodium chicken
broth

¾ teaspoon fennel seeds

½ teaspoon kosher salt

½ teaspoon freshly ground
black pepper

per serving: Calories 175;
Protein 7g; Carbohydrates
18g; Dietary Fiber 6g; Sugar
6g; Total Fat 9g; Saturated
Fat 5g; Sodium 289mg

green pea, lettuce, and fennel soup

I first had something similar to this in London during the Olympics. I really enjoyed it, especially the bit of a licorice flavor from the fennel. If you wouldn't think of putting lettuce in a soup, you should; it adds a light flavor and texture to go with the body and richness from the peas. A touch of butter rounds everything out. This is definitely a *green* soup. Serve it hot or at room temperature. *serves* 4

Melt the butter in a large heavy saucepan over medium heat. Add the fennel and shallots. Cover and cook, stirring occasionally, until the vegetables soften, 6 to 7 minutes. Add the lettuce and stir until it wilts, 1 to 2 minutes. Mix in the peas, broth, and 1 cup water. Bring the soup to a boil. Cover, reduce the heat to medium-low, and simmer until the vegetables are just tender, 5 to 6 minutes.

Puree the soup, in batches, in the blender until smooth, adding some fennel seeds to each batch. Combine the batches in a large bowl and return all of the soup to the same pot. Add the salt and pepper. Reheat the soup over low heat, thinning with a little water if it is too thick.

Ladle the soup into bowls. Garnish with a sprinkle of fennel fronds and serve.

2 pounds cherry tomatoes, stemmed

1 (12-ounce) bag frozen pearl onions, thawed

3 garlic cloves, smashed and peeled

1 tablespoon chopped fresh rosemary leaves

1½ teaspoons kosher salt

½ teaspoon freshly ground black pepper

3 tablespoons extra-virgin olive oil

3 cups low-sodium chicken broth

2 (8-ounce) skinless halibut fillets, cut into ½-inch pieces

3 tablespoons chopped fresh basil leaves

per serving: Calories 320; Protein 29g; Carbohydrates 19g; Dietary Fiber 4g; Sugar 12g; Total Fat 5g; Saturated Fat 3g; Sodium 613mg

roasted tomato soup with halibut

I like to roast the tomatoes and pearl onions together for this soup to get that smoky flavor and to enrich the sweetness of the tomatoes. Then I puree them in the blender with stock to make a delicate, almost creamy soup. Halibut has a great meatiness to it that pairs well with the tomatoes, though you could always substitute shrimp or chicken. Serve with some crusty bread if you're in the mood. *Serves 4*

Position an oven rack in the center of the oven and preheat the oven to 400°F. Line a heavy rimmed baking sheet with parchment paper.

In a medium bowl, combine the tomatoes, onions, garlic, rosemary, 1 teaspoon of the salt, and ¼ teaspoon of the pepper. Add the oil and toss until all of the ingredients are coated. Arrange the vegetables in a single layer on the prepared baking sheet. Roast until golden and tender, 40 to 45 minutes. Transfer the roasted vegetables (plus any cooking juices) to a blender. Add the chicken broth and blend until smooth.

Pour the tomato mixture into a large saucepan. Add the remaining ½ teaspoon salt and ¼ teaspoon pepper and bring to a simmer over medium heat. Add the halibut and cook until the fish is cooked through, 4 to 5 minutes. Stir in the basil.

Ladle the soup into shallow bowls and serve.

2 tablespoons olive oil

1 medium onion, chopped

2 celery stalks, chopped

½ teaspoon kosher salt

¼ teaspoon freshly ground black pepper

1 (12-ounce) package frozen artichoke hearts, thawed

2 cups vegetable broth

1 cup (packed) fresh spinach leaves

1 tablespoon chopped fresh mint

½ lemon, cut into 4 wedges

per serving: Calories 134; Protein 4g; Carbohydrates 15g; Dietary Fiber 7g; Sugar 5g; Total Fat 8g; Saturated Fat 1g; Sodium 279mg

artichoke soup with fresh mint

This is a light, fresh-tasting vegetarian/vegan soup with bright, clean flavors. The artichokes add texture and a lemony taste, while spinach brings its vibrant color. A little bit of mint at the end ties this all together and adds a refreshing note. *serves* 4

In a large saucepan, heat the oil over medium heat. Add the onion, celery, ¼ teaspoon of the salt, and the pepper. Cook the vegetables until just tender, about 4 minutes. Add the artichokes and broth and bring to a boil. Cover, reduce the heat to medium-low, and simmer until the artichokes are tender, about 12 minutes.

In a blender, puree the soup, 1 cup at a time, until very smooth, adding the spinach and chopped mint with the last cup. Return the puree to the saucepan. Mix in the remaining ¼ teaspoon salt. Reheat over low heat, thinning with water if too thick.

Ladle the soup into bowls. Squeeze 1 lemon wedge over each bowl of soup before serving.

vinaigrette

2 teaspoons cumin seeds

¼ cup extra-virgin olive oil

2 tablespoons plus
   1½ teaspoons apple
   cider vinegar

½ teaspoon kosher salt

½ teaspoon freshly ground
   black pepper

⅛ teaspoon ground
   cinnamon

⅛ teaspoon ground cloves

1 large shallot, finely chopped

salad

2 cups vegetable broth

1¼ cups quinoa

Vegetable oil cooking spray

1 (1¼-pound) eggplant, cut
   into ½-inch cubes

3 tablespoons extra-virgin
   olive oil

¼ teaspoon kosher salt

¼ teaspoon freshly ground
   black pepper

1 large apple, such as Honey
   Crisp or Golden Delicious,
   cut into ½-inch pieces

¾ cup walnut pieces,
   toasted (see Cook's Note,
   page 89)

½ cup unsweetened dried
   cranberries

1 large bunch of watercress

per serving: Calories 444;
Protein 11g; Carbohydrates
44g; Dietary Fiber 8g;
Sugar 10g; Total Fat 27g;
Saturated Fat 3g; Sodium
317mg

quinoa, roasted eggplant, and apple salad with cumin vinaigrette

Quinoa is my go-to grain these days because it is so satisfying and has a great texture. I love it in salads, especially this vegetarian/vegan one, which features Moroccan flavors. The eggplant adds body, the apple crunch and freshness, and the cumin warmth. This salad will keep for several days; spoon the salad over the watercress just before serving. *serves 6*

for the vinaigrette: Toast the cumin seeds in a heavy medium skillet over medium heat, stirring occasionally, until the seeds darken in color and become fragrant, 3 to 4 minutes. Turn the seeds out onto a plate and let cool for a minute or two. Grind the seeds fine in a small spice or coffee grinder. Whisk the oil, vinegar, salt, pepper, cinnamon, cloves, and 1½ teaspoons of the toasted cumin in a small bowl until thick and blended. Stir in the shallot.

for the salad: Position an oven rack in the center of the oven and preheat the oven to 400°F.

Bring the broth to a simmer in a heavy medium saucepan over medium-high heat. Mix in the quinoa. Reduce the heat to medium-low, cover, and simmer until the water is absorbed and the quinoa is tender, about 15 minutes. Turn off the heat and let the quinoa stand, covered, for 5 to 10 minutes. Transfer to a large bowl, let cool, and then fluff with a fork.

Meanwhile, spray a large rimmed baking sheet with vegetable oil cooking spray. On the baking sheet, toss the eggplant with the oil, salt, and pepper. Roast, stirring once, until tender and browned, about 30 minutes. Remove from the oven and let cool slightly, 5 minutes.

Add the vinaigrette, eggplant, apple, walnuts, and cranberries to the quinoa and toss to blend. Cover the bottom of a shallow platter with the watercress. Spoon the quinoa salad on top and serve immediately.

½ cup (4 ounces) mascarpone cheese, at room temperature

¼ cup whole-grain mustard

¼ cup honey

Grated zest of 1 large lemon

1 teaspoon kosher salt

½ teaspoon freshly ground black pepper

1½ packed cups arugula, chopped

2 cups shredded cooked skinless chicken breast

2 (9 x 12-inch) whole-wheat lavash breads

per serving: Calories 453; Protein 29g; Carbohydrates 48g; Dietary Fiber 3g; Sugar 21g; Total Fat 17g; Saturated Fat 8g; Sodium 629mg

chicken and honey-mustard pinwheels

I make these for Jade for lunch all the time—and for Todd, too, actually! They are creamy inside and pack a bit of everything into each bite: some protein, some greens, and some grains. They hold up beautifully in a lunch box alongside some carrot sticks. *serves 4*

In a medium bowl, mix together the mascarpone, mustard, honey, lemon zest, salt, and pepper. Stir in the arugula and chicken.

Divide the chicken mixture between the breads and spread it over the breads, leaving a ½-inch border. Starting at the longest edge, tightly roll up each bread like a jelly roll. Using a serrated knife, cut each roll into 8 pieces and serve.

per serving: Calories 400; Protein 26g; Carbohydrates 13g; Dietary Fiber 5g; Sugar 6g; Total Fat 28g; Saturated Fat 4g; Sodium 543mg

shrimp and avocado salad

A spin on the Los Angeles restaurant The Ivy's chopped California salad, this recipe uses fewer ingredients that still pack a lot of flavor so that it's easier to make at home. The salad only gets better as it sits overnight in the fridge, which means it is perfect to make ahead and pack for lunch. Butter lettuce holds it nicely—like a wrap—but you could just as easily serve it over leftover quinoa or brown rice. *serves* 4

for the salad: In a medium bowl, mix together ¼ cup of the olive oil, the soy sauce, garlic, lemon zest, parsley, chives, salt, and pepper. Add the shrimp and toss until coated. Refrigerate for 30 minutes.

Place a grill pan over medium-high heat or preheat a gas or charcoal grill.

Using a pastry brush, brush the zucchini halves with the remaining 1 teaspoon oil. Grill until tender, 4 to 5 minutes per side. Transfer to a cutting board. Grill the shrimp until pink and cooked through, 2 to 3 minutes per side. Transfer to the cutting board. When cool enough to handle, cut the zucchini and shrimp into ½-inch pieces.

for the dressing: In a small bowl, whisk together the oil, lemon juice, agave, mustard, salt, and pepper until smooth.

In a medium bowl, combine the zucchini, shrimp, and avocado. Add the dressing and gently toss until all the ingredients are coated. Using a slotted spoon, spoon the salad into the butter lettuce leaves.

panzanella

2 Japanese eggplants, halved lengthwise

2 medium zucchini, halved lengthwise

1 red bell pepper, cut into ¾-inch strips

1½ cups (6 ounces) frozen artichokes, thawed, halved

2 tablespoons extra-virgin olive oil

1 teaspoon kosher salt

¼ teaspoon freshly ground black pepper

1 (15-ounce) can chickpeas, rinsed and drained

10 jarred sun-dried tomatoes, drained and chopped

2 tablespoons chopped fresh basil leaves

2 tablespoons chopped fresh flat-leaf parsley leaves

2 tablespoons plus 2 teaspoons apple cider vinegar

2 tablespoons rinsed and drained capers

Grated zest of 1 large lemon

2 tablespoons fresh lemon juice (from 1 large lemon)

1 teaspoon light agave nectar

2 whole-wheat pita breads

pita and grilled vegetable panzanella

I have to admit this is a completely nontraditional panzanella, given that the bread is replaced by crispy pita chips served alongside. I like this fun and healthy twist on a classic recipe. The combo of the hearty veggies with the crunchy chips paired with a little yogurt sauce is my idea of a perfect light lunch. *serves 6*

for the panzanella: Put a grill pan over medium-high heat or preheat a gas or charcoal grill.

In a medium bowl, toss together the eggplants, zucchini, bell pepper, artichokes, oil, salt, and pepper. Grill the vegetables until grill-marked and tender, 3 to 4 minutes per side. Transfer to a cutting board. When cool enough to handle, chop the vegetables into ¾-inch pieces.

In a large bowl, toss together the grilled vegetables, chickpeas, sun-dried tomatoes, basil, parsley, vinegar, capers, lemon zest, lemon juice, and agave. Refrigerate for at least 30 minutes and up to 1 day before serving.

RECIPE CONTINUES

sauce

- ¼ cup plain low-fat (2%) Greek yogurt
- 1 tablespoon chopped fresh flat-leaf parsley
- 1½ teaspoons fresh lemon juice
- ¼ teaspoon apple cider vinegar
- ¼ teaspoon light agave nectar
- ¼ teaspoon kosher salt
- ⅛ teaspoon freshly ground black pepper

per serving: Calories 220; Protein 9g; Carbohydrates 37g; Dietary Fiber 12g; Sugar 6g; Total Fat 7g; Saturated Fat 1g; Sodium 490mg

Preheat the oven to 400°F.

Split the pita breads in half horizontally to make 4 rounds. Cut each round into sixths. Arrange the pita in a single layer on a heavy baking sheet. Bake until crisp, 7 to 8 minutes. Set aside to cool.

for the sauce: whisk together the yogurt, parsley, lemon juice, vinegar, agave, salt, and pepper in a small bowl until well combined.

To assemble, divide the vegetable panzanella among 6 plates. Add 4 pita chips to each plate and dollop the yogurt sauce on top.

croutons

3 (¾-inch-thick) slices country-style sourdough bread

1½ tablespoons extra-virgin olive oil

dressing

¼ cup extra-virgin olive oil

2 tablespoons dry white wine, such as pinot grigio

2 tablespoons honey

1 teaspoon whole-grain mustard

½ teaspoon kosher salt

½ teaspoon freshly ground black pepper

salad

2 (8-ounce) heads radicchio, halved and chopped into 1-inch pieces

3 cups baby arugula

2 ripe but firm Asian or Bosc pears, cored, halved, and cut lengthwise into ¼-inch-thick slices

¼ cup walnut pieces, toasted (see Cook's Note, page 89)

1 (2-ounce) chunk Parmesan cheese

per serving: Calories 473; Protein 12g; Carbohydrates 42g; Dietary Fiber 5g; Sugar 14g; Total Fat 29g; Saturated Fat 6g; Sodium 626mg

radicchio, pear, and arugula salad

I gave an Italian-style salad a California spin to make a light lunch. The radicchio is slightly bitter and the arugula has a little spiciness—both of which are complemented by the sweet delicate pear. Croutons and walnuts add crunch and Parmesan cheese infuses saltiness and a savory quality. This is one colorful, beautiful salad. *serves* 4

for the croutons: Place a grill pan over medium-high heat or preheat a gas or charcoal grill.

Brush the bread on each side with the olive oil. Grill until grill-marked and golden, 1 to 2 minutes per side. Cool slightly and then cut into ¾-inch cubes.

for the dressing: In a small bowl, whisk together the oil, wine, honey, mustard, salt, and pepper until smooth.

for the salad: In a large bowl, combine the radicchio, arugula, pears, walnuts, and croutons. Add the dressing and toss until coated. Using a vegetable peeler, shave the Parmesan cheese on top, and serve.

3 tablespoons extra-virgin olive oil

2 large or 4 small shallots, chopped

1 small red bell pepper, cut into ½-inch pieces

1 teaspoon kosher salt

½ teaspoon freshly ground black pepper

1½ cups quinoa

¼ cup dry white wine, such as pinot grigio

1½ cups low-sodium chicken broth

1 medium cucumber, peeled, seeded, and cut into ½-inch pieces

1 packed cup arugula, chopped

½ cup chopped fresh mint leaves

Grated zest of 1 lemon

½ cup slivered almonds, toasted (see Cook's Note) and coarsely chopped

per serving: Calories 480; Protein 14g; Carbohydrates 54g; Dietary Fiber 7g; Sugar 3g; Total Fat 23g; Saturated Fat 3g; Sodium 332mg

quinoa pilaf

Rather than make a classic rice pilaf, which I learned to prepare in cooking school, I take this dish in a more modern California direction using quinoa as the main ingredient. And instead of relegating this to side-dish territory, I add even more flavors—cucumber, arugula, mint, lemon zest, and almonds—so the pilaf becomes a true meal all on its own. Serve this hot or at room temperature. Leftovers are good chilled, straight from the fridge, too. *serves 4*

In a large saucepan or a high-sided skillet, heat 2 tablespoons of the oil over medium-high heat. Add the shallots and cook until soft, about 2 minutes. Add the bell pepper, salt, and pepper. Cook until the bell pepper is tender, 5 minutes. Make a space in the center of the vegetables and add the remaining 1 tablespoon oil. Add the quinoa and cook, stirring constantly, until coated with oil, about 2 minutes.

Pour in the wine and cook until all of the liquid has evaporated, about 2 minutes. Pour in the broth and bring to a boil. Cover the pan and simmer until all of the broth has been absorbed and the quinoa is tender, about 15 minutes. Remove from the heat, cover, and let sit for 10 minutes.

Stir the cucumber, arugula, mint, lemon zest, and almonds into the quinoa and serve.

cook's note
To toast the almonds, arrange in a single layer on a baking sheet. Bake in a preheated 350°F oven until lightly toasted, 6 to 8 minutes. Cool completely before using.

rice

2 cups low-sodium chicken broth

1½ tablespoons chopped fresh thyme

¾ cup short-grain brown rice

¾ cup wild rice

vegetables

2 tablespoons extra-virgin olive oil

7 ounces frozen pearl onions, thawed

1 teaspoon kosher salt

½ teaspoon freshly ground black pepper

4 ounces portobello mushrooms (about 1½ large), thinly sliced

4 ounces Brussels sprouts, thinly sliced

¼ cup hazelnuts, toasted (see Cook's Note, page 90) and coarsely chopped

per serving: Calories 277; Protein 8g; Carbohydrates 42g; Dietary Fiber 4g; Sugar 3g; Total Fat 9g; Saturated Fat 1g; Sodium 231mg

brown and wild rice with brussels sprouts

I first developed this recipe as a gluten-free Thanksgiving stuffing and it ended up being something I loved so much I didn't want to save it for just once a year. Now I make it all the time for lunch. The different textures and nutty flavors of brown rice and wild rice complement each other so well. This dish is great warm or at room temperature! *serves 6*

for the rice: In a heavy saucepan or Dutch oven, bring the broth, ¼ cup water, and the thyme to a boil over medium-high heat. Add the brown rice and wild rice. Cover the saucepan, lower the heat, and simmer until the rice is tender but still chewy, about 30 minutes. Turn off the heat and allow the rice to stand for 10 minutes. Fluff with a fork.

for the vegetables: Meanwhile, in a large nonstick skillet, heat the oil over medium-high heat. Add the onions and season with ½ teaspoon of the salt and ¼ teaspoon of the pepper. Cook, stirring occasionally, until light golden, about 5 minutes. Add the mushrooms, ½ teaspoon of the salt, and ⅛ teaspoon of the pepper. Cook until softened, about 8 minutes. Add the Brussels sprouts and the remaining ½ teaspoon salt and ⅛ teaspoon pepper. Cook until the vegetables are tender, about 5 minutes.

Transfer the vegetable mixture to the saucepan of cooked rice. Add the hazelnuts. Toss until all the ingredients are mixed. Transfer to a large bowl and serve.

quinoa

2 cups low-sodium chicken broth

1½ cups quinoa

dressing

¼ cup extra-virgin olive oil

2 teaspoons grated lemon zest

¼ cup fresh lemon juice (from 1 large lemon)

¾ cup chopped fresh basil leaves

¼ cup chopped fresh flat-leaf parsley leaves

1 tablespoon chopped fresh thyme

½ teaspoon kosher salt

¼ teaspoon freshly ground black pepper

2 (4-ounce) cans boneless, skinless salmon, drained and flaked

per serving: Calories 401; Protein 15g; Carbohydrates 46g; Dietary Fiber 4g; Sugar 1g; Total Fat 19g; Saturated Fat 3g; Sodium 244mg

herbed quinoa

 gf df

One of the ways I enhance flavor in food without adding salt and fat is with fresh herbs. This recipe has a ton of them! Not only do they add amazing flavor, they also lend their beautiful color here: The white flecks of quinoa mingle with bits of green herbs and the pretty pink of salmon. *serves* 4

for the quinoa: In a medium saucepan, bring the chicken broth and quinoa to a boil over medium-high heat. Reduce the heat so that the broth simmers, cover the pan, and cook until all the liquid is absorbed, 12 to 15 minutes. Transfer the quinoa to a large bowl.

for the dressing: Meanwhile, in a small bowl, whisk together the olive oil, lemon zest, lemon juice, basil, parsley, thyme, salt, and pepper.

Pour the dressing over the quinoa and toss with the salmon until all of the ingredients are coated.

My weekly indulgence is a manicure. I have had a standing appointment at the same salon with the same manicurist for fifteen years. It's funny that people always ask me now about my nails and what polish I wear, because I have a secret to confess: Long, long ago, I was a nail biter. But, when I got a manicure, I liked how pretty my nails looked and I didn't bite them. It helped me cure my bad habit, but I never thought it would become such a thing!

On camera, I wear a light shade so that the food is the star and my nails don't detract from it (but the polish does hide any carrot stains or other job hazards). My favorite translucent pinks for filming are Essie Ballet Slipper, Angel Food Cake, and OPI Bubble Bath. These days Jade has me mixing it up: I'll embellish my ring fingers with something a bit special. I stay in the same color family so it's a little hit of fun but nothing too crazy!

dressing

⅓ cup extra-virgin olive oil

⅓ cup apple cider vinegar

1 tablespoon frozen apple juice concentrate, thawed

2 garlic cloves, minced

1½ teaspoons minced fresh thyme

¼ teaspoon kosher salt

¼ teaspoon freshly ground black pepper

salad

2 ounces goat cheese, crumbled into ½-inch chunks (¼ cup)

4 (2-inch-diameter) red or golden beets, tops trimmed, peeled

6 ounces green beans, ends trimmed, cut into 2-inch lengths

1 teaspoon extra-virgin olive oil

Pinch of kosher salt

Pinch of freshly ground black pepper

1 head butter lettuce, cut into 1-inch pieces

2 packed cups baby arugula

½ large Granny Smith apple, sliced

per serving: Calories 305; Protein 6g; Carbohydrates 17g; Dietary Fiber 5g; Sugar 10g; Total Fat 24g; Saturated Fat 6g; Sodium 217mg

beet and marinated goat cheese salad

Beets are one of my favorites because they're sweet but still good for you. The combo of beets and goat cheese is classic California. I like to add green beans to the mix for texture, along with arugula for a little kick. The dressing relies on cider vinegar for a tart sweetness that complements the beets. *serves 4*

Preheat the oven to 425°F.

for the dressing: In a small bowl, whisk together all of the ingredients.

for the salad: Put the goat cheese in a medium bowl and drizzle with just enough of the dressing to moisten. Refrigerate until ready to serve.

Wrap each beet in foil. Place the beets on a baking sheet and roast in the oven until tender, about 50 minutes. When the beets are almost tender, put the green beans in a pie dish. Add the oil, salt, and pepper, and toss to coat. Roast the green beans until crisp-tender, about 8 minutes. Remove the beets and green beans from the oven. Unwrap the foil from the beets and set them aside until cool enough to handle. Cut each beet into 6 to 8 wedges.

In a large bowl, combine the lettuce and arugula. Add the apple slices and green beans. Top with the beet wedges. Sprinkle the cheese on top. Pour the dressing over the salad, toss until coated, and serve.

wheat berries

2 cups soft white wheat berries, rinsed and drained

4 cups vegetable broth

½ teaspoon kosher salt

dressing

Grated zest of ½ orange

½ cup fresh orange juice

⅓ cup extra-virgin olive oil

2 tablespoons light agave nectar

¼ packed cup fresh mint leaves, finely chopped

½ teaspoon kosher salt

½ teaspoon freshly ground black pepper

10 medium strawberries, hulled and chopped into ¼-inch pieces

2 ounces goat cheese, crumbled (¼ cup)

per serving: Calories 406; Protein 13g; Carbohydrates 54g; Dietary Fiber 9g; Sugar 9g; Total Fat 17g; Saturated Fat 4g; Sodium 289mg

wheat berries with strawberries

Wheat berries take a while to cook. So I make a batch on the weekend and then use it throughout the week. I love the slightly crunchy texture. This is my take on a rice salad but with new players. The citrusy dressing goes well with sweet strawberries and tangy goat cheese. Delicious at any temperature! *serves* 4

for the wheat berries: In a large saucepan, combine the wheat berries, broth, 4 cups water, and the salt. Bring to a boil over high heat. Reduce the heat so that the liquid simmers, cover the pan, and cook until the wheat berries are tender, 60 to 70 minutes. Drain the wheat berries in a colander and set aside to cool, about 15 minutes. Transfer to a salad bowl.

for the dressing: In a medium bowl, whisk together the orange zest, orange juice, oil, agave, mint, salt, and pepper until smooth.

Pour the dressing over the wheat berries and add the strawberries and goat cheese. Toss until all of the ingredients are coated.

salad

2 cups (½-inch) diced cooked skinless chicken breast

1 large mango, peeled, seeded, and cut into small cubes (about 1½ cups)

2 (4-ounce) Persian or pickling cucumbers, scrubbed and cut into small cubes

1 (15-ounce) can black beans, rinsed and drained

⅔ cup sliced almonds, toasted (see Cook's Note, page 116)

½ lightly packed cup fresh mint leaves

dressing

Grated zest of 1 large lime

⅓ cup fresh lime juice (from 2 to 3 large limes)

¼ cup honey

1 tablespoon Dijon mustard

2 tablespoons chopped fresh mint leaves

1 teaspoon kosher salt

½ teaspoon freshly ground black pepper

⅛ teaspoon cayenne pepper

⅓ cup creamy almond butter

per serving: Calories 367; Protein 24g; Carbohydrates 38g; Dietary Fiber 6g; Sugar 20g; Total Fat 16g; Saturated Fat 2g; Sodium 392mg

chicken, mango, and black beans with lime-almond dressing

Todd loves this tropical version of a chicken salad. The mango, beans, and nutty, tangy mayo-free dressing make it positively addictive. This is a tough one to put down—it's that good.

serves 6

for the salad: In a large bowl, combine the chicken, mango, cucumbers, black beans, almonds, and mint leaves.

for the dressing: In a small bowl, whisk together the lime zest, lime juice, honey, mustard, mint, salt, black pepper, and cayenne pepper. Add the almond butter and whisk until the dressing is smooth and thickened.

Add the dressing to the salad and toss to combine. Serve chilled.

1 head Bibb or Boston lettuce

5 ounces white button mushrooms (about 4 large), brushed clean

1 small fennel bulb, top trimmed

4 large red radishes, trimmed

6 tablespoons extra-virgin olive oil

Grated zest of 1 large lemon

2½ tablespoons fresh lemon juice (from 1 large lemon)

2 tablespoons chopped fresh chives

½ teaspoon kosher salt

½ teaspoon freshly ground black pepper

4 hard-boiled eggs (see Cook's Note), chopped into ½-inch pieces

per serving: Calories 300; Protein 8g; Carbohydrates 8g; Dietary Fiber 3g; Sugar 3g; Total Fat 26g; Saturated Fat 5g; Sodium 240mg

fennel, radish, and chive salad

Topping this fresh, raw salad with chopped hard-boiled eggs turns it into a perfect lunch. The colors here are stunning: red radish, white fennel, green chives, yellow egg. This crunchy, refreshing salad is great in summer. *serves* 4

Tear the lettuce into bite-size pieces and put in a large bowl. Using a knife or a mandoline, cut the mushrooms, fennel, and radishes into ⅛-inch-thick slices. Add to the bowl with the lettuce.

Whisk the oil, lemon zest, lemon juice, chives, salt, and pepper in a small bowl to blend. Add the dressing to the salad and toss to blend.

Divide the salad among 4 plates, top with the chopped egg, and serve.

cook's note
To make hard-boiled eggs, put the eggs in a saucepan. Add enough water to cover by 1 inch. Bring to a boil and cook for 3 minutes. Cover the pan, turn off the heat, and let sit for 9 minutes. Cool immediately in a bowl of ice water.

quinoa

1½ cups quinoa

2 cups low-sodium chicken broth

½ teaspoon kosher salt

Grated zest of 1 large lemon

dressing

¼ cup safflower or grapeseed oil

3 tablespoons light agave nectar

2 tablespoons fresh lime juice (from about 2 large limes)

1 tablespoon apple cider vinegar

1 tablespoon ground cumin

1 teaspoon kosher salt

¼ teaspoon freshly ground black pepper

1 (15-ounce) can black beans, rinsed and drained

1 (15-ounce) can hominy, rinsed and drained

¼ cup chopped fresh cilantro leaves

per serving: Calories 368; Protein 11g; Carbohydrates 57g; Dietary Fiber 8g; Sugar 9g; Total Fat 12g; Saturated Fat 1g; Sodium 466mg

quinoa with black beans and hominy

 gf df

This Southwestern-style salad was inspired by a recent trip to Arizona. Hominy is like large, puffy, white corn with a nice bite to it. If you love the flavor of popcorn and the texture of pasta, this is a great whole grain to check out. Along with beans, it's one of the few canned foods I really enjoy. The cumin adds warmth here and a hint of spice, and it goes well with bright lime and the slightly caramel flavor of agave in the dressing. *Serves 6*

for the quinoa: In a medium saucepan, bring the quinoa, chicken broth, salt, and lemon zest to a boil over medium-high heat. Reduce the heat, cover the pan, and simmer until the liquid has been absorbed and the quinoa is tender, about 20 minutes. Remove the pan from the heat and allow to cool for 10 minutes.

for the dressing: In a small bowl, whisk together the oil, agave, lime juice, vinegar, cumin, salt, and pepper until smooth.

In a serving bowl, combine the quinoa, black beans, hominy, and cilantro. Add the dressing and toss until coated. Serve warm or at room temperature.

dressing

⅓ cup extra-virgin olive oil

2 tablespoons apple cider vinegar

1½ teaspoons smoked paprika

1 teaspoon kosher salt

½ teaspoon freshly ground black pepper

couscous

1 tablespoon extra-virgin olive oil

1⅓ cups (8 ounces) whole-wheat pearl couscous

½ teaspoon kosher salt

salad

2 cups grape or cherry tomatoes, halved

1 cup jarred roasted red bell peppers, drained and coarsely chopped

2 packed cups baby spinach leaves, coarsely chopped

½ cup chopped fresh flat-leaf parsley leaves

¼ cup chopped fresh mint leaves

⅓ cup slivered almonds, toasted (see Cook's Note, page 116)

4 ounces feta cheese, coarsely crumbled (1 cup)

per serving: Calories 384; Protein 10g; Carbohydrates 33g; Dietary Fiber 6g; Sugar 1g; Total Fat 24g; Saturated Fat 5g; Sodium 544mg

whole-wheat pearl couscous salad with smoked paprika

The smoked paprika dressing makes this dish. I would put that dressing on everything if I could! The couscous absorbs it and becomes a beautiful terra-cotta color with great depth of flavor. Crunchy fresh veggies are a nice contrast in this hearty salad, which is good at room temperature or chilled. *serves 6*

for the dressing: In a small bowl, whisk together the olive oil, vinegar, smoked paprika, salt, and pepper until smooth.

for the couscous: In a large saucepan, heat the olive oil over medium-high heat. Add the couscous and cook, stirring frequently, until the couscous is golden, 4 to 5 minutes. Add 2 cups water and the salt and bring to a boil. Reduce the heat to medium-low. Cover and simmer until the couscous is just tender and the liquid is absorbed, 9 to 10 minutes. Uncover and set aside to cool slightly.

for the salad: In a large bowl, mix together the tomatoes, bell peppers, spinach, parsley, mint, almonds, and feta. Add the couscous and the dressing. Toss until all the ingredients are coated.

ceviche

1 (10-ounce) halibut fillet, skinned and cut into ½-inch cubes

Grated zest of 1 large lemon

½ cup fresh lemon juice (from 2 large lemons)

¼ cup fresh lime juice (from 3 large limes)

1 teaspoon kosher salt

½ teaspoon freshly ground black pepper

salad

2 tablespoons extra-virgin olive oil

2 tablespoons fresh lime juice (from 2 large limes)

1 teaspoon light agave nectar

¼ teaspoon kosher salt

⅛ teaspoon freshly ground black pepper

1 large avocado, cut into ½-inch cubes

2 medium tomatoes, seeded and chopped into ½-inch pieces

3 scallions, white and pale green parts only, finely sliced

1 small jalapeño, finely diced

2 tablespoons chopped fresh flat-leaf parsley leaves

¼ cup crumbled baked tortilla chips

per serving: Calories 274; Protein 17g; Carbohydrates 13g; Dietary Fiber 4g; Sugar 4g; Total Fat 18g; Saturated; Fat 3g; Sodium 229mg

halibut ceviche salad with avocado salsa

 gf df

I love the vibrant citrus flavor of ceviche and how it plumps up the texture of fresh fish. This is a great light weekend lunch when I am having the girls over. A sprinkling of crushed tortilla chips adds a bit of crunch and pizzazz. *serves 4*

for the ceviche: In an 8-inch square glass or ceramic baking dish, mix together the halibut, lemon zest, lemon juice, lime juice, salt, and pepper. Cover the dish and refrigerate for 3 hours, stirring once during that time.

for the salad: In a medium bowl, mix together the olive oil, lime juice, agave, salt, and pepper until smooth. Add the avocado, tomatoes, scallions, jalapeño, and parsley. Toss until coated.

Divide the salad among 4 small salad bowls. Drain the ceviche and spoon on top of the salad. Garnish with the crumbled tortilla chips before serving.

8 ounces dried buckwheat soba noodles

dressing

3 tablespoons creamy almond butter

3 tablespoons reduced-sodium soy sauce

3 tablespoons extra-virgin olive oil

¼ cup fresh lime juice (from 3 large limes)

1 tablespoon sesame oil

1 tablespoon honey

1 (1-inch) piece of fresh ginger, peeled and coarsely chopped

2 teaspoons wasabi paste

salad

1 (1½-pound) head napa cabbage, cored and shredded

1 red bell pepper, thinly sliced

3 scallions, white and green parts, thinly sliced

1 hothouse cucumber, peeled, halved lengthwise, and thinly sliced

½ cup slivered almonds, toasted (see Cook's Note, page 116)

3 tablespoons black sesame seeds

per serving: Calories 562; Protein 18g; Carbohydrates 66g; Dietary Fiber 5g; Sugar 10g; Total Fat 28g; Saturated Fat 3g; Sodium 873mg

soba noodle salad

This is my Asian spin on a pasta salad, loaded with crunchy vegetables, though instead of a peanut dressing I go for an almond one. The longer this salad sits in the fridge, the longer the flavors blend, the more the noodles soak up the dressing, and the better it all becomes. If you haven't tried buckwheat, it's a nutty whole grain that makes chewy noodles; if you are gluten-free, make sure to find a brand that's 100 percent buckwheat.

serves 4

Bring a large pot of salted water to a boil over high heat. Add the noodles and cook, stirring occasionally, until tender but still firm to the bite, 4 to 5 minutes. Rinse well in cold water, drain, and put in a serving bowl.

for the dressing: In a blender, combine the almond butter, soy sauce, olive oil, lime juice, sesame oil, 2 tablespoons water, the honey, ginger, and wasabi paste. Blend until smooth.

for the salad: Pour the dressing over the pasta. Add the cabbage, bell pepper, scallions, cucumber, and almonds. Toss until all of the ingredients are coated. Garnish with the sesame seeds and serve.

salad

1 cup quick-cooking bulgur (cracked wheat)

½ teaspoon fresh lemon juice, plus 1 lemon, quartered

¼ teaspoon kosher salt

6 large kale leaves

4 medium plum tomatoes, cut into ½-inch dice

3 scallions, white and light green parts only, chopped

1 large Persian cucumber, cut into ⅓-inch dice

10 kalamata olives, pitted and quartered

4 peperoncini, drained, stemmed, and finely chopped

vinaigrette

Grated zest of 2 lemons

¼ cup fresh lemon juice (from 1 large lemon)

1 large garlic clove, minced

2 teaspoons dried oregano

1 teaspoon kosher salt

½ teaspoon freshly ground black pepper

⅔ cup extra-virgin olive oil

per serving: Calories 535; Protein 7g; Carbohydrates 38g; Dietary Fiber 10g; Sugar 4g; Total Fat 41g; Saturated Fat 6g; Sodium 596mg

greek tabbouleh salad with kale

All you need is a little hot water to "cook" this amazing tabbouleh. Then I mix it with olives, peperoncini, kale, crunchy cucumbers, and a lemony garlic vinaigrette. It couldn't be simpler. Make it ahead and enjoy it for a few days. *Serves 4*

for the salad: Combine the bulgur, lemon juice, and salt in a medium bowl. Mix in 3 cups very hot tap water. Let stand overnight, until the bulgur is softened but still chewy.

Drain the bulgur very well, tapping the sieve to release excess water. Transfer to a large bowl.

Remove the stems and center ribs from the kale leaves. Set aside 4 of the prettiest leaves and finely chop the remaining 2 leaves.

Add the finely chopped kale, 2 of the tomatoes, the scallions, cucumber, olives, and peperoncini to the bulgur and toss to blend.

for the vinaigrette: In a small bowl, whisk together the lemon zest, lemon juice, garlic, oregano, salt, pepper, and oil until combined.

Pour the vinaigrette over the bulgur and stir to combine. Let stand, stirring occasionally, for at least 30 minutes and, refrigerated, for up to 2 hours for the flavors to blend.

Line large shallow bowls with the 4 reserved kale leaves. Spoon the tabbouleh into the bowls. Sprinkle with the remaining 2 tomatoes, garnish with lemon wedges, and serve.

packing tip

This is my number one packing tip and the way I ready myself for any trip, big or small: I plan all of my outfits in advance and then pack them in one-gallon-size zip-top bags in my suitcase. The accessories go in the bags, too, and then I write on each one which shoe to wear with it and what day or night the outfit is for. I press out all the air, meaning I can get more into my suitcase, and the bags then protect my clothes in so many ways: The clothes stay pressed and dry (whether from rain or spills in cargo)—and they never smell like airplane (or jet fuel). An extra couple of baggies go in for dirty laundry.

Best of all, this system also prevents me from overpacking, meaning my suitcase is only as heavy as it needs to be.

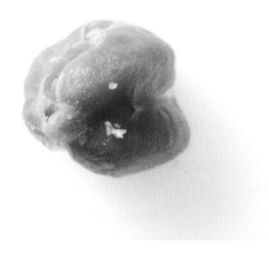

LAVASH CHIPS with Creamy Tomato-Basil Dip

ROASTED RED PEPPER HUMMUS in Cucumber Cups

AVOCADO HUMMUS with Crispy Pita Chips

POPCORN with Herbes de Provence and Smoked Sea Salt

CINNAMON KETTLE CORN

SPICED COCKTAIL NUTS

SMOKED ALMONDS

CRISPY CHICKPEAS

ROSEMARY CASHEWS AND SUNFLOWER SEEDS

HOMEMADE CRANBERRY NUT GRANOLA

CHEWY GRANOLA BARS

BAKED KALE AND SWEET POTATO CHIPS

SPICED APPLE CHIPS

FRUIT SALAD with Honey-Lime Syrup

snacks

1 (9 x 12-inch) piece of whole-wheat lavash bread

1 tablespoon extra-virgin olive oil

1 cup tomato-basil sauce

¼ cup (2 ounces) crumbled creamy Gorgonzola cheese, at room temperature

¼ cup (2 ounces) mascarpone cheese, at room temperature

per serving: Calories 159; Protein 5g; Carbohydrates 12g; Dietary Fiber 2g; Sugar 0g; Total Fat 10g; Saturated Fat 4g; Sodium 327mg

lavash chips with creamy tomato-basil dip

Lavash is an unleavened Mediterranean bread that's super flat, even flatter than pita. It makes great chips. The dip evolved from a pasta sauce I used to like as a kid: In a pinch one time, with guests on their way, I repurposed the ingredients as a dip and everyone loved it! Leftovers make a nice accompaniment to chicken. *Serves 6*

Preheat the oven to 375°F.

Cut the lavash into 1 x 4-inch strips. Arrange on a rimmed baking sheet in a single layer. Drizzle with the olive oil. Bake until crisp, 5 to 6 minutes. Set aside to cool.

In a medium saucepan, bring the tomato sauce to a simmer over medium heat. Cook for 5 minutes. Remove the pan from the heat and whisk in the gorgonzola and mascarpone until incorporated.

Pour the dip into a serving bowl and serve the chips alongside.

1 (15-ounce) can cannellini beans, rinsed and drained

½ cup diced jarred roasted red bell peppers

1 tablespoon tahini (sesame seed paste)

1 large garlic clove, peeled

2 teaspoons fresh lemon juice

½ teaspoon ground cumin

½ teaspoon kosher salt

Pinch of cayenne pepper (optional)

2 hothouse cucumbers, ends trimmed

Fresh flat-leaf parsley, cilantro, or mint leaves, for serving (optional)

per serving: Calories 50; Protein 3g; Carbohydrates 7g; Dietary Fiber 2g; Sugar 1g; Total Fat 1g; Saturated Fat 0g; Sodium 106mg

roasted red pepper hummus in cucumber cups

This is a nice alternative to chips and dip—one that features no white carbs. The cucumber cup is a cute container for this pretty pink hummus. I make these before company is coming over and then leave them in the fridge. Sometimes a whole bunch are missing because Jade has snuck in there and eaten them!

serves 6

In a food processor, combine the beans, roasted peppers, tahini, garlic, lemon juice, cumin, salt, and cayenne pepper, if using. Blend until smooth, scraping down the sides of the bowl if needed. Transfer the hummus to a small bowl.

Run the tines of a fork down the length of each cucumber several times, turning to make ridges about ⅛ inch deep in the skin all the way around. Cut the cucumbers crosswise into 1-inch rounds, for a total of at least 12. Using the smaller end of a melon baller or a small round measuring spoon, scoop out part of the center of each cucumber round to form a hollow. Use a small spoon (or a pastry bag fitted with a star tip) to fill each cup with hummus, mounding it slightly over the top. Tuck a small fresh parsley leaf into the side of the filling as a garnish, if desired.

Arrange the cups on a platter and serve.

pita chips

⅓ cup extra-virgin olive oil

Grated zest of 2 large limes (optional)

1 teaspoon chili powder

2 whole-wheat pita breads, split in half to make 4 circles of bread

½ teaspoon kosher salt

¼ teaspoon freshly ground black pepper

hummus

1 large (12-ounce) avocado, coarsely chopped

½ packed cup arugula

1 (15-ounce) can cannellini beans, rinsed and drained

⅓ cup fresh flat-leaf parsley leaves

2 tablespoons fresh lemon juice (from 1 large lemon)

1 garlic clove, smashed

1 teaspoon kosher salt

¼ teaspoon freshly ground black pepper

2 tablespoons extra-virgin olive oil

per serving: Calories 301; Protein 4g; Carbohydrates 19; Dietary Fiber 5g; Sugar 1g; Total Fat 24g; Saturated Fat 4g; Sodium 405mg

avocado hummus with crispy pita chips

This is one of our favorite afternoon/after-school snacks at home, Jade included. I often put this out as an appetizer with drinks when friends are coming over for dinner. In fact, this bright green dip is so versatile that I'll also serve it as a side to a simple piece of grilled fish. Instead of buying pita chips, which are expensive and can be loaded with fat and other additives, you can make your own at home. *Serves 6*

for the pita chips: Position an oven rack in the center of the oven and preheat the oven to 350°F.

In a small bowl, whisk together the oil, lime zest, if using, and chili powder. Using a pastry brush, brush the mixture on both sides of the bread circles. Sprinkle the breads with the salt and pepper. Cut each bread half into 8 wedges and put on a baking sheet in a single layer. Bake until crisp and golden, 15 to 18 minutes.

for the hummus: In the bowl of a food processor, combine the avocado, arugula, beans, parsley, lemon juice, garlic, salt, and pepper. Pulse until the mixture is coarsely chopped. With the machine running, gradually add the olive oil and process until the mixture is creamy.

Spoon the hummus into a serving bowl and serve the pita chips alongside.

½ cup safflower or grapeseed oil

2 large garlic cloves, crushed

1½ teaspoons dried herbes de Provence, crumbled

½ cup popcorn kernels

1½ teaspoons smoked sea salt

per serving: Calories 166; Protein 2g; Carbohydrates 9g; Dietary Fiber 2g; Sugar 0g; Total Fat 14g; Saturated Fat 1g; Sodium 375mg

popcorn with herbes de provence and smoked sea salt

This is a great grab-and-go snack to put in your bag for a hunger attack. Todd, Jade, and I all love it. Todd is a huge popcorn fan. In fact, I had never eaten much of it until I met him. This is his favorite, a tasty light spin on what you can buy at the store. The smoked salt is my secret ingredient here to add a lot of satisfying flavor. *makes 8 cups ; serves 8*

In a small saucepan, combine ¼ cup of the oil, the garlic, and the herbes de Provence. Cook over medium-low heat until the garlic is aromatic, about 3 minutes. Remove the pan from the heat and let stand while making the popcorn.

Combine the remaining ¼ cup oil and the popcorn kernels in a heavy large pot. Cover and cook over medium-high heat, shaking the pan occasionally, until almost all the kernels pop, 3 to 5 minutes. Transfer the popcorn to a large bowl.

Remove the garlic cloves from the oil mixture and discard. Pour the flavored oil over the hot popcorn and then sprinkle with the smoked salt. Toss until the popcorn is coated. Serve hot or at room temperature.

Vegetable oil cooking spray

¼ cup safflower or grapeseed oil

½ cup popcorn kernels

1 cup turbinado sugar, such as Sugar in the Raw

1 teaspoon pure vanilla extract

½ teaspoon ground cinnamon

per serving: Calories 199; Protein 2g; Carbohydrates 33g; Dietary Fiber 2g; Sugar 23g; Total Fat 7g; Saturated Fat 1g; Sodium 10mg

cinnamon kettle corn

There's a stand at the farmer's market that makes warm, sweet caramel corn that Jade absolutely loves. I decided one day to make my own, which is a slightly healthier take without all the butter. (Remember: While it's always a good thing to support local farmers, just because you buy something at the farmer's market doesn't mean it's automatically good for you!) The truth is that we all love this sweet little pick-me-up.

makes about 8 cups ; serves 8

Line a baking sheet with wax or parchment paper. Spray a large bowl with vegetable oil cooking spray.

Combine the oil and popcorn kernels in a large heavy saucepan. Cover and cook over medium-high heat, shaking the pan occasionally, until the kernels have popped, about 8 minutes. Transfer the popcorn to the prepared bowl.

Heat a 12-inch nonstick skillet over medium heat. Add the sugar and cook, stirring occasionally, until the sugar melts, about 8 minutes. Remove the skillet from the heat and carefully stir in the vanilla and cinnamon.

Carefully drizzle the melted sugar mixture over the popcorn. Using 2 wooden spoons, toss until the popcorn is coated with the sugar mixture. Transfer the mixture to the prepared baking sheet and let cool for 10 minutes. Break the caramel corn into 1- to 2-inch pieces before serving or storing.

Vegetable oil cooking spray

1 large egg white

1 cup roasted and salted
   almonds

1 cup hazelnuts, toasted (see
   Cook's Note, page 90)

1 cup walnut halves, toasted
   (see Cook's Note, page 89)

¼ cup sugar

1 tablespoon Madras curry
   powder

1½ teaspoons ground cumin

1¼ teaspoons garlic salt

½ teaspoon cayenne pepper

½ teaspoon ground
   cardamom

¼ teaspoon ground
   cinnamon

per serving: Calories 322;
Protein 9g; Carbohydrates
15g; Dietary Fiber 5g; Sugar
8g; Total Fat 28g; Saturated
Fat 2g; Sodium 217mg

spiced cocktail nuts

I put this out as my cocktail appetizer when I have people over.
And then leftovers go in a plastic bag in my purse; I especially
like to take these with me on the plane when I travel for a little hit
of satisfying protein. These are tastier than plain nuts and I know
exactly what is in this mix! *serves 8*

Position an oven rack in the center of the oven and preheat the
oven to 250°F. Spray a baking sheet liberally with vegetable oil
cooking spray.

In a large bowl, whisk the egg white until frothy. Add the almonds,
hazelnuts, and walnuts and stir until coated. In a small bowl,
combine the sugar, curry powder, cumin, garlic salt, cayenne
pepper, cardamom, and cinnamon. Sprinkle the sugar mixture
over the nuts and toss until coated.

Arrange the nuts in a single layer on the prepared baking sheet.
Bake until golden and fragrant, about 45 minutes. Set aside to
cool for 1 hour.

Using a metal spatula, remove the nuts from the baking sheet.
Break the nuts into bite-sized pieces and put in serving bowls.

3 cups raw almonds

3 tablespoons extra-virgin olive oil

1½ tablespoons smoked sea salt

per serving: Calories 347; Protein 11g; Carbohydrates 11g; Dietary Fiber 7g; Sugar 3g; Total Fat 30g; Saturated Fat 2g; Sodium 938mg

smoked almonds

If you thought almonds were boring, just wait until you taste these! This recipe is all about the smoked salt, my favorite ingredient these days. It turns ordinary almonds into something extraordinary. While this recipe is a bit higher in sodium, the flavor just isn't the same if you use less salt. So don't eat these every single day. Throw these in your bag from time to time to mix things up come snacktime. *serves 8*

Preheat the oven to 375°F.

In a medium bowl, combine the almonds, olive oil, and smoked salt. Toss until well coated. Pour the nut mixture onto a baking sheet in an even layer. Roast in the oven until the almonds are aromatic, crunchy, and slightly golden, 10 to 12 minutes. Let cool before serving or storing.

cook's note
For a nice spicy kick of flavor, add ½ teaspoon crushed red pepper flakes. For an herb aroma and flavor, add 2 teaspoons herbes de Provence.

Vegetable oil cooking spray

2 (15-ounce) cans chickpeas, rinsed and drained

2 tablespoons extra-virgin olive oil

2 teaspoons smoked sea salt

per serving: Calories 153; Protein 7g; Carbohydrates 23g; Dietary Fiber 8g; Sugar 0g; Total Fat 6g; Saturated Fat 1g; Sodium 751mg

crispy chickpeas

These are super-fun. The first time I had this very Mediterranean snack, the chickpeas took the place of croutons in a salad. I thought they were brilliant—until I realized that they were deep-fried! So I tinkered with the idea at home to come up with a recipe in which they're baked instead; the perfect combination of olive oil and smoked salt does the trick. These are super-crunchy and remind me of corn nuts, which I adored as a child. *serves 6*

Position an oven rack in the center of the oven and preheat the oven to 350°F. Spray a baking sheet with vegetable oil cooking spray.

Put the chickpeas on a clean kitchen towel or several sheets of paper towel and dry thoroughly. In a medium bowl, toss the chickpeas with olive oil to coat. Sprinkle with the smoked salt and toss again. Transfer in an even layer to the prepared baking sheet.

Bake, shaking the pan halfway through the baking time, until the chickpeas are crunchy, 50 minutes to 1 hour. Let cool for at least 1 hour; the chickpeas will become crunchier as they cool. These are best eaten within 1 day.

Vegetable oil cooking spray

1 large egg white

½ teaspoon kosher salt

2 tablespoons pure maple syrup

1 tablespoon plus 1 teaspoon dried rosemary

¼ teaspoon cayenne pepper

2 cups raw cashew nuts

1 cup raw shelled sunflower seeds

per serving: Calories 277; Protein 9g; Carbohydrates 16g; Dietary Fiber 2g; Sugar 4g; Total Fat 21g; Saturated Fat 3g; Sodium 83mg

rosemary cashews and sunflower seeds

I always make these crunchy golden nuts around the holidays. The sweetness of the caramelized maple syrup and the smoky piney flavor of rosemary combine to make the perfect seasonal bite. *serves 8*

Preheat the oven to 325°F. Spray a heavy baking sheet with vegetable oil cooking spray.

In a medium bowl, whisk the egg white and salt just until foamy. Add the maple syrup, rosemary, and cayenne pepper. Stir in the nuts and sunflower seeds and toss until coated.

Spread the nut mixture on the prepared baking sheet in a single layer. Bake until the nuts are crisp and brown, 25 to 30 minutes, stirring halfway through. Let cool before serving or storing.

⅓ cup pumpkin seeds

¼ cup shelled sunflower seeds

Vegetable oil cooking spray

⅔ cup pure maple syrup

⅓ cup honey

¼ cup unsweetened cranberry juice

1½ teaspoons ground cinnamon

2 cups old-fashioned rolled oats

½ cup chopped roasted and salted almonds

¼ teaspoon fine sea salt

1 cup unsweetened dried cranberries

per serving: Calories 310; Protein 7g; Carbohydrates 51g; Dietary Fiber 5g; Sugar 30g; Total Fat 11g; Saturated Fat 1g; Sodium 97mg

homemade cranberry nut granola

My first instinct was to put this in the breakfast chapter but I truly eat it all day long. I keep a big glass jar of it at home and dip into it as needed, even after dinner for a quick something sweet. The crunch factor is so satisfying and I love the chewy cranberries. Store-bought granolas can be loaded with white sugar and fat. This one is a slightly lighter option. Make it and give as gifts—as a housewarming present, for the neighbors at the holidays, or for any occasion. *serves 8*

Preheat the oven to 350°F.

Spread the pumpkin seeds and sunflower seeds on a baking sheet. Bake until lightly toasted, 8 to 10 minutes. Set aside to cool.

Reduce the oven temperature to 325°F. Spray a baking sheet with vegetable oil cooking spray.

In a small bowl, whisk together the maple syrup, honey, cranberry juice, and cinnamon. In a medium bowl, mix together the oats, almonds, pumpkin seeds, sunflower seeds, and salt. Pour the maple mixture over the oat mixture and stir until combined.

Spread the mixture onto the prepared baking sheet. Bake for 20 minutes. Remove the baking sheet from the oven. Stir in the cranberries and bake until the mixture begins to brown, an additional 10 to 15 minutes. Let cool completely before serving or storing.

Vegetable oil cooking spray

¾ cup honey

⅓ cup safflower or grapeseed oil

3 large egg whites, at room temperature

½ teaspoon pure vanilla extract

2 cups old-fashioned rolled oats

½ cup flaxseed meal

2 teaspoons ground cinnamon

¼ teaspoon ground nutmeg

1 teaspoon fine sea salt

½ cup chopped almonds

½ cup walnut pieces

6 dried apricots, chopped into ½-inch pieces

⅓ cup unsweetened dried cranberries

⅓ cup raisins

per bar: Calories 231; Protein 6g; Carbohydrates 28g; Dietary Fiber 4g; Sugar 15g; Total Fat 13g; Saturated Fat 2g; Sodium 135mg

chewy granola bars

Everybody loves granola bars, but a lot of time we buy expensive sugary ones at the grocery store and throw them in our bag without thinking. This is a homemade take. I love the smell of these as they're baking. Egg whites and dried fruit make them chewy—that's my favorite thing about good granola bars.

makes 16 bars

Position an oven rack in the center of the oven and preheat the oven to 350°F. Spray a 9 x 13-inch glass or ceramic baking dish with vegetable oil cooking spray. Line the bottom and sides of the baking dish with parchment paper. Spray the parchment paper with vegetable oil cooking spray, too.

In a large bowl, whisk together the honey, oil, egg whites, and vanilla extract until smooth. In a medium bowl, combine the oats, flaxseed, cinnamon, nutmeg, and salt. Pour the oat mixture into the honey mixture and stir until the ingredients are coated. Stir in the almonds, walnuts, apricots, cranberries, and raisins. Transfer the mixture to the prepared baking dish. Using a spatula, press the mixture into the pan.

Bake until light golden, about 35 minutes. Put the baking dish on a wire rack to cool for 25 to 30 minutes. Cut into 1-inch-square bars and store in an airtight container for up to 5 days.

1 medium sweet potato
(8 ounces)

2 tablespoons extra-virgin
olive oil

¾ teaspoon kosher salt

¼ teaspoon freshly ground
black pepper

3 large kale leaves

per serving: Calories 131;
Protein 2g; Carbohydrates
17g; Dietary Fiber 2g; Sugar
4g; Total Fat 7g; Saturated
Fat 1g; Sodium 239mg

baked kale and sweet potato chips

With a color combination as stunning as this, no one is looking for the fried potato chips. Kale is like popcorn—salty and crunchy and disappears in your mouth. The sweet potatoes are mellow and crunchy. *serves 4*

Position an oven rack in the center of the oven and preheat the oven to 350°F.

Using a mandoline slicer or a sharp knife, slice the potato into ⅛-inch-thick slices. Put in a bowl and drizzle with 1 tablespoon of the olive oil. Toss well. Arrange in a single layer (without overlapping) on parchment-lined baking sheets.

Bake for 12 minutes. Turn the slices over and continue to bake, checking every 2 minutes, until brown and crisp, 6 to 8 minutes longer. Season the chips with ½ teaspoon of the salt and ⅛ teaspoon of the pepper.

Remove the thick stem from the kale leaves and discard. Cut the leaves into 2- to 3-inch pieces. Put in a bowl and drizzle with the remaining 1 tablespoon olive oil. Toss well. Arrange the kale in a single layer on parchment-lined baking sheets.

Bake the kale until crisp and slightly dark on the edges, 10 to 12 minutes. Season with the remaining ¼ teaspoon salt and ⅛ teaspoon pepper.

Let the chips cool before serving.

Vegetable oil cooking spray

2 tablespoons sugar

1 teaspoon ground cinnamon

¼ teaspoon kosher salt

2 (6- to 7-ounce) tart apples, such as Granny Smith

per serving: Calories 53; Protein 0g; Carbohydrates 14g; Dietary Fiber 2g; Sugar 12g; Total Fat 0g; Saturated Fat 0g; Sodium 47mg

spiced apple chips

These are just amazing. They crackle and then melt in your mouth. You need very thin slices of apple; I recommend buying an inexpensive Japanese mandoline for the job. The slices are baked and then sprinkled with cinnamon sugar. I use super-tart apples, such as Granny Smiths, which are available year-round.

serves 4

Position racks at the top and bottom of the oven and preheat the oven to 300°F. Line 2 large (12 x 18-inch) baking sheets with parchment paper. Lightly coat the parchment with vegetable oil cooking spray.

Stir the sugar, cinnamon, and salt in a small bowl until blended.

Stand each apple upright on a cutting board. Cut ¼ inch vertically off the right and left sides of each apple. Set a mandoline for cutting ¹⁄₁₆-inch-thick slices. Place 1 apple, a cut side down, on the mandoline. Using the guard, carefully cut slices until you reach the core. Turn the apple over and cut slices off the remaining side until you reach the core again. Arrange the apple slices in a single layer (without overlapping) on a prepared baking sheet. Repeat with the second apple. Sprinkle the apple slices generously with the cinnamon sugar.

Bake the apple slices for 30 minutes. Reverse the sheets from top to bottom in the oven and also rotate them from back to front. Bake until the slices curl at the edges, feel crisp or almost crisp, and are deep golden, 10 to 15 minutes longer. Pull the parchment and apple slices onto a counter and let cool completely, 20 to 30 minutes. The chips will crisp more as they cool.

syrup

Grated zest of 3 large limes

¼ cup fresh lime juice

3½ tablespoons honey

fruit

½ (2-pound) cantaloupe, seeded and cut into 1-inch chunks

12 medium strawberries, hulled and sliced

1 cup green or red seedless grapes, halved

2 kiwi, peeled and cut into ½-inch pieces

1 cup blueberries

Fresh mint leaves, for serving

per serving: Calories 170; Protein 2g; Carbohydrates 44g; Dietary Fiber 5g; Sugar 38g; Total Fat 1g; Saturated Fat 0g; Sodium 11mg

fruit salad with honey-lime syrup

This is an anytime recipe: It makes a nice snack, a light breakfast, or a summery dessert on a warm night. This syrup can be used on any fruit combo, any time of year. When Jade hasn't eaten well during the day and wants something sweet, I make this for her. She's satisfying her sweet tooth and eating something good for her at the same time. *Serves 4*

for the syrup: In a small saucepan, combine the lime zest, lime juice, honey, and 3 tablespoons water. Bring to a boil over medium heat. Reduce the heat and simmer for 4 minutes. Set aside to cool, about 20 minutes.

for the fruit: In a serving bowl, combine the melon, strawberries, grapes, kiwi, and blueberries. Pour the syrup over the fruit and toss to coat. Let the fruit salad sit for at least 15 minutes or up to 1 day, refrigerated, before serving, garnished with mint leaves.

dinner

SALMON HAND ROLLS

SHRIMP, AVOCADO, AND MANGO ROLLS

VEGETABLE ROLLS with Chile Yogurt Sauce

MY MOM'S VEGETABLE "MEATLOAF" with Checca Sauce

GRILLED SALMON AND PINEAPPLE with Avocado Dressing

NOODLE PAELLA

HALIBUT with Artichoke and Olive Caponata

WHOLE ROASTED CHICKEN with Vegetable Bolognese

GRILLED SCALLOPS with Orange-Scented Quinoa

GRILLED HERBED TOFU with Avocado Cream

SOUTHERN ITALIAN–STYLE HERBED CHICKEN

CALIFORNIA TURKEY CHILI

VEGETARIAN CHILI VERDE

CHRISTMAS SEAFOOD SALAD

SALMON with Lemon, Capers, and Rosemary

GARLIC-ROASTED CHICKEN AND ROOT VEGETABLES

SLICED PORK TENDERLOIN with Citrus Slaw

SWISS CHARD ROLLS with Wild and Brown Rice and Indian Spices

GRILLED STRIPED BASS with Tomato and Bell Pepper Sauce

SOLE with Lemon-Basil Pesto

PORK TENDERLOIN with Honey-Mustard Sauce

LENTIL BURGERS with Lemon-Basil Mayonnaise

BAKED SALMON with Arugula Salsa Verde

SALMON with Basil and Chive Tzatziki

MAHIMAHI with Mango-Vanilla Sauce

ROASTED VEGETABLES with Chipotle Cream over Crispy Pita

BROILED SOLE with Mustard-Chive Sauce

GRILLED CHICKEN CUTLETS with Fresh Apple-Mango Chutney

STUFFED RED BELL PEPPERS with Whole-Wheat Couscous and Avocado Sauce

WHOLE-WHEAT LINGUINE with Shrimp, Asparagus, and Cherry Tomatoes

LEMON-CUMIN CHICKEN with Mint and Spinach Pesto

8 thin asparagus spears,
trimmed to 5 inches long

1 (12-ounce) center-cut
skinless sushi-grade
salmon fillet, finely
chopped

2 tablespoons sesame oil

2 tablespoons soy sauce

¼ teaspoon wasabi paste

½ cup finely chopped fresh
mint leaves

4 toasted nori sheets, cut in
half lengthwise

Short-Grain Brown Sushi Rice
(recipe follows)

per serving (includes rice):
Calories 312; Protein 23g;
Carbohydrates 27g; Dietary
Fiber 2g; Sugar 1g; Total
Fat 13g; Saturated Fat 2g;
Sodium 700mg

salmon hand rolls

You don't need any special equipment to make these—no sushi mat or anything like that—and almost every grocery store these days has nori (seaweed). If the idea of raw salmon makes you uncomfortable, you can substitute chopped cooked shrimp, or check out the vegan variations that follow. So you have no reason not to try this recipe! A refreshing cucumber salad would complement this dish for a great, light dinner. Serve with wasabi, pickled ginger, and soy sauce, if desired.

Makes 8 hand rolls; serves 4

Steam the asparagus spears until crisp-tender, about 3 minutes. Set aside to cool.

In a medium bowl, mix together the salmon, sesame oil, soy sauce, wasabi paste, and mint leaves.

Put a sheet of nori, shiny side down, on a work surface. Spoon ¼ cup of the rice on the left side of the nori. Using wet fingers, form the rice into a 3-inch square, leaving a ½-inch border. Spoon about 2 tablespoons of the salmon mixture, diagonally, in a ½-inch-wide strip, on the rice, with the top of the salmon mixture facing the top-left corner. Put an asparagus spear on top of the salmon. Starting with the bottom-left corner, roll the nori over the filling. Continue to roll, ice cream cone–fashion, working toward the right corner of the nori. Seal the edge of the hand roll with water or a few grains of the cooked rice. Repeat with the remaining ingredients.

Arrange on a serving platter and serve.

short-grain brown sushi rice

If you are making the Shrimp, Avocado, and Mango Rolls on page 163 and need four cups of rice, this recipe doubles easily.

MAKES 2 CUPS

⅔ cup short-grain brown rice
2 tablespoons seasoned rice vinegar

In a medium saucepan, bring 1⅓ cups water to a boil over high heat. Stir in the rice and cover the pan with a tight-fitting lid. Reduce the heat to low and simmer until the liquid is absorbed, about 50 minutes. Remove the pan from the heat and let sit, still covered, for 10 minutes.

Sprinkle the vinegar over the rice and mix with a fork. Allow the rice to cool completely before using.

vegan hand rolls

This is definitely a dish you can play with and make your own. Some great vegan filling combinations include:

- smoked tofu with thinly sliced red onion and microgreens or sprouts

- strips of cucumber, radish, carrot, and avocado

- pickled ginger, avocado, and sesame seeds

1 pound large shrimp, cooked and finely chopped

3 tablespoons egg-free mayonnaise, such as Vegenaise

2 teaspoons fresh lemon juice

1 tablespoon light agave nectar

1 teaspoon wasabi paste

8 toasted nori sheets

4 cups Short-Grain Brown Sushi Rice (page 161)

½ small avocado, thinly sliced

½ small mango, peeled and thinly sliced

½ small red bell pepper, thinly sliced

special equipment: a bamboo sushi mat

per serving: Calories 435; Protein 25g; Carbohydrates 61g; Dietary Fiber 5g; Sugar 8g; Total Fat 11g; Saturated Fat 2g; Sodium 234mg

shrimp, avocado, and mango rolls

I love ordering a roll with these kinds of flavors in a sushi restaurant but they can have lots of extra hidden calories in them. So I re-created the recipe at home, holding on to the flavors that I like so much, but lightening everything up; I opt for brown rice instead of white, use a lot less mayo (I go for egg-free mayo, actually), and omit white sugar and the usual fried garnish. I do still serve them with wasabi, pickled ginger, and soy sauce, for guests to customize the flavors. Give these a try because I think you will love them! *makes 8 rolls; serves 4*

In a medium bowl, mix together the shrimp, mayonnaise, lemon juice, agave, and wasabi.

Put the sushi mat on a counter with the slats running horizontally. Put a sheet of nori, shiny side down, on the mat. Using wet fingers, spread ½ cup of the rice evenly over the nori to form a rectangle slightly smaller than the nori. Arrange ¼ cup of the shrimp mixture along the center of the rice. Top the shrimp mixture with 4 thin avocado slices, 4 thin mango slices, and 4 thin bell pepper slices. Using the sushi mat as a guide, fold the rice over the filling and roll into a log. Repeat with the remaining ingredients.

Place the logs, seam sides down, on a cutting board. Using a sharp, damp knife, slice each log into 6 pieces (re-wet the knife after each slice). Arrange the rolls on a serving platter and serve.

cook's note
For spicier rolls, substitute 2 seeded and thinly sliced jalapeños for the bell pepper.

sauce

⅓ cup plain nonfat (0%) Greek yogurt

1 tablespoon Asian chile sauce

1 tablespoon fresh lemon juice

1 tablespoon plus 1½ teaspoons fish sauce

1 garlic clove, minced

1 tablespoon light agave nectar

rolls

4 ounces dried soba (buckwheat) noodles

1 red bell pepper, thinly sliced

½ yellow bell pepper, thinly sliced

1 large carrot, shredded

8 (8-inch) rice paper rounds

8 butter lettuce leaves, ribs removed

8 fresh basil leaves

8 fresh mint leaves

per serving: Calories 110; Protein 4g; Carbohydrates 24g; Dietary Fiber 1g; Sugar 4g; Total Fat 0g; Saturated Fat 0g; Sodium 408mg

vegetable rolls with chile yogurt sauce

These vegetable rolls are anything but boring. The creamy, spicy, lemony, delicious sauce flavors the veggies, making them irresistible. The secret ingredient is fish sauce, which can be found in most grocery stores these days and keeps in the fridge for a long time. It adds a salty bite that you just can't replace with salt alone. It's kind of like the Asian version of anchovies in Italian cooking, transforming vegetables into something crave-worthy. If you can't find the rice paper rounds, which can be bought in Asian specialty markets and some supermarkets, just use the lettuce leaves alone as your wrappers. *Makes 8 rolls; serves 4*

for the sauce: In a medium bowl, mix together the yogurt, chile sauce, lemon juice, fish sauce, garlic, and agave.

for the rolls: Bring a large saucepan of water to a boil over high heat. Add the noodles and cook until tender, about 8 minutes. Drain and rinse with cold water. Using scissors, cut the noodles into 2-inch pieces. Add the noodles, red bell pepper, yellow bell pepper, and carrot to the yogurt sauce and toss until coated.

Lay a damp kitchen or paper towel on a work surface. Soak a rice paper round in warm water until softened, 20 to 30 seconds. Put the rice paper on the damp towel. Lay a lettuce leaf in the middle of the rice paper and spoon ⅓ cup of the noodle mixture on top. Put 1 basil leaf and 1 mint leaf on top of the noodle mixture. Roll the rice paper around the filling and seal the ends with a little water. Repeat with the remaining ingredients.

If not serving immediately, drape the finished vegetable rolls with damp paper towels, wrap with plastic wrap, and store in the refrigerator for up to 6 hours.

sauce

1 pint cherry tomatoes, halved

3 scallions, white and pale green parts only, coarsely chopped

3 garlic cloves, chopped

8 fresh basil leaves

3 tablespoons extra-virgin olive oil

1 teaspoon kosher salt

½ teaspoon freshly ground black pepper

lentil loaf

Vegetable oil cooking spray

2 tablespoons extra-virgin olive oil

1 small white onion, finely chopped

1 medium carrot, shredded

1 celery stalk, thinly sliced

10 ounces fresh baby spinach (about 4 cups)

1 (15-ounce) can cooked lentils, rinsed and drained

2 cups cooked brown rice

1 cup shredded low-fat mozzarella cheese

½ cup frozen corn kernels, thawed

⅓ cup chopped fresh basil leaves

2 large eggs, lightly beaten

1 large egg white, lightly beaten

1 teaspoon kosher salt

½ teaspoon freshly ground black pepper

2 medium tomatoes, sliced

my mom's vegetable "meatloaf" with checca sauce

My Mom, Veronica, is pretty much a vegetarian these days. When she invites us over for "meatloaf," this is what we get—and I like it a lot; in fact, even Todd does. The lentils and the brown rice make it hearty while at the same time kind of fluffy and light. My favorite part about it is the fresh tomato sauce, which is almost like a salsa. *Checca* is a Southern Italian term for this fresh sauce, which is called by different names in different regions. Some of it goes into the lentil loaf and the rest is served alongside. *serves* 6

for the sauce: In a food processor, combine the cherry tomatoes, scallions, garlic, basil, oil, salt, and pepper. Pulse the tomatoes until they are coarsely chopped, being careful not to puree them. Transfer the sauce to a bowl.

for the lentil loaf: Preheat the oven to 350°F. Spray a 10 x 4½-inch loaf pan with vegetable oil cooking spray.

Meanwhile, heat a large skillet over medium heat. Add 1 tablespoon of the olive oil. Add the onion, carrot, and celery and cook until tender, about 5 minutes. Transfer to a large bowl to cool slightly. Reserve the skillet.

In the same large skillet, cook the spinach over medium heat until the spinach wilts, about 3 minutes. Drain and let cool slightly. Squeeze the excess liquid from the spinach. Transfer the spinach to a cutting board and coarsely chop. Add to the onion mixture.

Add the lentils, brown rice, ¾ cup of the mozzarella, the corn, basil, eggs, egg white, salt, pepper, and ¾ cup of the sauce to the cooled onion mixture. Spoon the mixture into the prepared

per serving: Calories 388;
Protein 17g; Carbohydrates
41g; Dietary Fiber 11g; Sugar
7g; Total Fat 19g; Saturated
Fat 5g; Sodium 631mg

pan. Arrange the sliced tomatoes in 2 rows over the lentil mixture,
covering the top completely. Sprinkle with the remaining ¼ cup
mozzarella and drizzle with the remaining 1 tablespoon olive oil.

Bake until the loaf is heated through and the topping is melted
and starting to brown, 30 to 35 minutes. Let cool for 15 minutes.
Slice the loaf (still in the pan) into 1-inch slices, arrange on plates,
and serve with the remaining sauce.

- 2 tablespoons extra-virgin olive oil
- 1½ teaspoons chopped fresh basil leaves, plus some sprigs for garnish
- 1½ teaspoons chopped fresh chives
- 1 teaspoon chopped fresh tarragon leaves, plus some sprigs for garnish
- ½ teaspoon kosher salt
- ½ teaspoon freshly ground black pepper
- 4 (4-ounce) salmon fillets with skin, each about 1 inch thick
- 4 (½-inch-thick) round slices of pineapple, preferably fresh (see Cook's Note)
- Avocado Dressing (recipe follows)

per serving (includes dressing): Calories 364; Protein 27g; Carbohydrates 13g; Dietary Fiber 2g; Sugar 10g; Total Fat 23g; Saturated Fat 3g; Sodium 246mg

grilled salmon and pineapple with avocado dressing

Pineapple replaces a starch in this dish while also adding sweetness and a little acidity, both of which are great with salmon and make a nice match for fresh herbs. This dish is absolutely stunning to look at. The pink salmon sits over a warm, smoky bed of grilled golden pineapple. This is a really great way, if you're going to have people over on a weeknight, to keep things simple but make something impressive. It's not your ordinary salmon dish but it's not so complicated that you can't handle it on a weeknight. *serves* 4

Place a grill pan over medium-high heat or preheat a gas or charcoal grill.

In a small bowl, whisk the oil, chopped basil, chives, chopped tarragon, salt, and pepper to blend. Brush the salmon and the pineapple slices with the herb mixture.

Put the salmon and the pineapple on the grill. Cook the salmon until barely cooked through and still pink inside, about 4 minutes per side. Cook the pineapple until slightly charred, 3 to 4 minutes per side.

Transfer 1 pineapple slice to each plate and arrange a piece of salmon slightly overlapping it. Spoon 2 tablespoons of the avocado dressing over each piece of fish. Garnish with fresh herb sprigs and serve.

cook's note
If using canned pineapple, make sure to blot it dry very well before grilling it.

RECIPE CONTINUES

avocado dressing

MAKES ½ CUP

½ avocado, diced

2 tablespoons chopped fresh basil leaves

1 tablespoon finely chopped fresh chives

1½ teaspoons finely chopped fresh tarragon leaves

1 small garlic clove, finely chopped

1 tablespoon extra-virgin olive oil

1½ teaspoons fresh lemon juice

⅛ teaspoon anchovy paste

⅛ teaspoon kosher salt

⅛ teaspoon freshly ground black pepper

Combine all of the ingredients in a food processor. Add
2 tablespoons water and process until smooth. Cover the
dressing and let stand for at least 15 minutes and up to 1 hour
for the flavors to blend.

3 tablespoons extra-virgin olive oil

1 pound boneless, skinless chicken breast halves, cut into ¾-inch pieces

¾ teaspoon kosher salt

¾ teaspoon freshly ground black pepper

1 medium fennel bulb, chopped

1 medium red bell pepper, diced

1 small onion, chopped

6 large garlic cloves, thinly sliced

3 (8-ounce) bottles clam juice

1 (15-ounce) can diced tomatoes with juice

3 dried bay leaves

1 teaspoon smoked paprika

¼ teaspoon crumbled saffron

⅛ teaspoon cayenne pepper

8 ounces whole-wheat spaghetti, broken into 1-inch pieces

12 small clams, such as Manila, scrubbed

12 large shrimp, peeled and deveined

⅓ cup chopped fresh flat-leaf parsley leaves

per serving: Calories 362; Protein 30g; Carbohydrates 40g; Dietary Fiber 8g; Sugar 5g; Total Fat 10g; Saturated Fat 2g; Sodium 646mg

noodle paella

In Spain, there's paella made with rice, and then there's paella made with noodles, which I also love. This is my simpler, lighter version, which keeps the fun of the traditional recipe but makes it doable at home—on a weeknight, even. The saffron, smoked paprika, clams, and shrimp preserve the spirit of a paella.

serves 6

In a 5-quart saucepan or Dutch oven, heat the oil over medium-high heat. Add the chicken and season with ¼ teaspoon of the salt and ¼ teaspoon of the black pepper. Cook until the chicken is no longer pink on the outside, 3 to 4 minutes. Using a slotted spoon, transfer the chicken to a medium bowl.

Add the fennel, bell pepper, onion, and garlic to the pan. Season with ¼ teaspoon of the salt and ¼ teaspoon of the pepper. Cook until just tender, about 5 minutes. Add the clam juice, tomatoes with their juices, bay leaves, paprika, saffron, and cayenne pepper. Bring the mixture to a simmer. Add the spaghetti and cook, stirring occasionally, until almost tender, about 9 minutes.

Return the chicken to the pan. Bring the sauce to a simmer. Add the remaining ¼ teaspoon salt and remaining ¼ teaspoon pepper. Add the clams and shrimp. Cover and cook until the clams open, the shrimp are pink and cooked through, and the chicken is cooked through, 4 to 5 minutes. Discard any unopened clams along with the bay leaves.

Mix in the parsley and serve.

caponata

¼ cup extra-virgin olive oil

1 small red onion, chopped

½ teaspoon kosher salt

½ teaspoon freshly ground black pepper

1 celery stalk, chopped

8 ounces frozen artichoke hearts, thawed and cut into 1-inch pieces

1 (14½-ounce) can diced tomatoes with juices

8 pitted kalamata olives, halved

3 tablespoons raisins

¼ cup red wine vinegar

1 tablespoon sugar

½ tablespoon capers, rinsed and drained

halibut

4 (4-ounce) skinless center-cut halibut fillets, each about 1 inch thick

3 tablespoons extra-virgin olive oil

½ teaspoon kosher salt

½ teaspoon freshly ground black pepper

3 tablespoons chopped fresh flat-leaf parsley leaves, for garnish

per serving: Calories 456; Protein 27; Carbohydrates 20g; Dietary Fiber 6g; Sugar 12g; Total Fat 30g; Saturated Fat 4g; Sodium 714mg

halibut with artichoke and olive caponata

This is a sweet and tangy chunky sauce that's a spin on the traditional Sicilian caponata; my version swaps out artichokes for the eggplant and bell peppers but still has raisins, capers, and vinegar. This flavor combination is stellar with seafood, brightening up fish, especially for those who are not big fish fans. Halibut is meaty and a good match for this bold sauce. *serves 4*

for the caponata: In a large skillet, heat the olive oil over medium-high heat. Add the onion and season with the salt and pepper. Cook until softened, about 3 minutes. Add the celery and artichoke hearts and cook until soft and the artichokes are lightly browned, 3 to 4 minutes. Add the tomatoes and their juices, the olives, and raisins to the pan. Simmer over medium-low heat, stirring frequently, until the mixture thickens, about 25 minutes. Stir in the vinegar, sugar, and capers.

for the halibut: Put a nonstick grill pan over medium-high heat or preheat a gas or charcoal grill. (See Cook's Note.)

Drizzle the halibut on both sides with the olive oil and season on both sides with the salt and pepper. Grill until the flesh flakes easily with a fork, 3 to 4 minutes per side.

Put the halibut on plates and top with the caponata. Garnish with the parsley and serve.

cook's note

The halibut can also be roasted for 10 to 12 minutes in a preheated 400°F oven.

chicken

1 (4½- to 5-pound) chicken, rinsed and patted dry

1 teaspoon kosher salt

½ teaspoon freshly ground black pepper

2 tablespoons extra-virgin olive oil

bolognese

1 ounce dried porcini mushrooms

1½ cups low-sodium chicken broth, hot

2 medium carrots, peeled and coarsely chopped

1 medium onion, coarsely chopped

1 red bell pepper, coarsely chopped

2 garlic cloves, smashed and peeled

2 tablespoons extra-virgin olive oil

1 tablespoon chopped fresh thyme leaves

1 tablespoon chopped fresh oregano leaves

¾ teaspoon kosher salt

½ teaspoon freshly ground black pepper

6 ounces assorted mushrooms, such as button, cremini, or stemmed shiitake (about 1½ cups), chopped

½ cup red wine, such as merlot or cabernet sauvignon

2 tablespoons tomato paste

½ cup mascarpone cheese, at room temperature

per serving: Calories 616; Protein 49g; Carbohydrates 12g; Dietary Fiber 3g; Sugar 4g; Total Fat 39g; Saturated Fat 11g; Sodium 501mg

whole roasted chicken with vegetable bolognese

While the chicken roasts—and nothing smells better than that on a Sunday—you can make the vegetable Bolognese. The great thing is you don't have to worry about the chicken being dry or flavorless; it just can't happen with this robust sauce made from mushrooms, red wine, and mascarpone. *Serves 6*

for the chicken: Position an oven rack in the center of the oven and preheat the oven to 400°F. Season the chicken with the salt and pepper and rub with the olive oil. Roast until a meat thermometer inserted into the thickest part of the thigh registers 160°F, about 1 hour and 15 minutes. Let the chicken rest for 15 minutes.

for the bolognese: Meanwhile, soak the dried porcini mushrooms in the hot broth until softened, 20 minutes. Strain the mushrooms and broth, reserving each separately.

In a food processor, combine the carrots, onion, bell pepper, and garlic. Pulse until the vegetables are finely chopped.

In a Dutch oven or large saucepan, heat the oil over medium-high heat. Add the chopped vegetables, the thyme, oregano, salt, and pepper. Cook until slightly softened, 6 minutes. Add the porcini and fresh mushrooms and cook until the mushrooms are soft, about 5 minutes. Pour in the wine and cook, stirring frequently, until most of the liquid has evaporated, about 5 minutes. Add the reserved broth and the tomato paste and stir until dissolved. Simmer over low heat until the liquid has reduced by half and the vegetables are tender, 25 to 30 minutes. Remove from the heat and stir in the mascarpone cheese.

Carve the chicken into thin slices and arrange on a platter. Spoon the sauce over the chicken and serve.

tips for eating out

I love eating in restaurants and trying new dishes. They can be such a source of inspiration in your cooking. But eating out all the time, such as when I am on the road, for example, or filming a show, can be a minefield. You're not in control of portion sizes or exact ingredients.

RESTAURANT PORTION

REASONABLE PORTION

Here are a few tips I use to make sure I don't overindulge in restaurants, which can throw me off balance and affect how I feel:

1 At dinner, I order two appetizers instead of an appetizer and a main course; entrées tend to be just too big in restaurants. I go for a vegetarian salad or soup and then something with some protein.

2 If I don't like the options under the appetizers, I order a main course but ask the server to bring only half of the portion to the table and to pack up the other half in a container to take home.

3 I find salads are sometimes overdressed in restaurants, so I always ask for dressing on the side. In fact, I often ask to have olive oil and lemon wedges instead of dressing so I can dress the salad to my liking—and eliminate any extraneous ingredients.

4 I always try to eat before getting on a plane and not on the plane. Foods served on board tend to have a lot of fat and sodium in them to make them taste better because your taste buds get dulled at high altitude. At the very least, most airports have a Starbucks these days where I can get oatmeal cooked with hot water that I can then doctor with an olive oil packet from my purse and a pinch of salt. That, plus the almonds that I always carry with me, can keep me going on a flight until I land.

quinoa

1½ cups quinoa

Grated zest of 1 large orange

1 teaspoon kosher salt

scallops

1½ pounds (1½- to 2-inch) scallops (16 to 20)

3 tablespoons extra-virgin olive oil

2 teaspoons kosher salt

½ teaspoon freshly ground black pepper

dressing

¼ cup extra-virgin olive oil

¼ cup fresh orange juice (from about 1 large orange)

2 tablespoons fresh lemon juice (from 1 large lemon)

1 teaspoon kosher salt

½ teaspoon freshly ground black pepper

1 (15-ounce) can chickpeas, drained and rinsed

⅓ cup chopped fresh flat-leaf parsley leaves

special equipment: 12 (8-inch) wooden skewers, soaked in water for 30 minutes to prevent scorching

per serving: Calories 441; Protein 28g; Carbohydrates 46g; Dietary Fiber 7g; Sugar 1g; Total Fat 17g; Saturated Fat 2g; Sodium 838mg

grilled scallops with orange-scented quinoa

This is a light yet very satisfying dish. Scallops are rich and meaty, so you don't need to serve a lot of them to do the trick. Chickpeas add some texture and body to the quinoa to make it more substantial and the orange zest infuses a nice bright citrusy flavor into the dish, flecking the grain with its pretty color.

serves 6

for the quinoa: In a medium saucepan, bring 2 cups water and the quinoa, orange zest, and salt to a boil over medium-high heat. Reduce the heat so that the mixture simmers. Cover the pan and cook until all the liquid has been absorbed, 10 to 12 minutes. Fluff with a fork, cover the pan, and let the quinoa sit for 10 to 12 minutes.

for the scallops: Place a grill pan over medium-high heat or preheat a gas or charcoal grill.

Thread 3 scallops onto a skewer. Thread another skewer (alongside the first) through the scallops about ½ inch apart to make flipping the skewers easier. Repeat with the remaining scallops and skewers to make 6 skewers in total. Drizzle with the olive oil and season with the salt and pepper. Grill until cooked through, 2 to 3 minutes per side.

for the dressing: In a small bowl, whisk together the olive oil, orange juice, lemon juice, salt, and pepper until smooth.

Put the quinoa into a large serving bowl. Add the dressing, chickpeas, and parsley. Toss until coated. Arrange the grilled scallops on top and serve.

tofu

- 1 (12-ounce) container extra-firm tofu, drained and patted dry
- 2 tablespoons extra-virgin olive oil
- 1 tablespoon dried herbes de Provence
- ¾ teaspoon kosher salt
- ¼ teaspoon freshly ground black pepper

avocado cream

- 1 ripe avocado
- ⅓ cup extra-virgin olive oil
- Grated zest of 1 large lime
- 1 tablespoon fresh lime juice (from 1 large lime)
- ½ cup vegetable broth
- ½ cup packed fresh flat-leaf parsley leaves
- 1 garlic clove, smashed and peeled
- ½ teaspoon kosher salt
- ¼ teaspoon freshly ground black pepper

per serving: Calories 388; Protein 10g; Carbohydrates 7g; Dietary Fiber 4g; Sugar 1g; Total Fat 36g; Saturated Fat 6g; Sodium 391mg

grilled herbed tofu with avocado cream

I don't eat a lot of tofu, but when I do, this is one of my favorite ways to eat it. When you grill tofu, it gets a nice smoky crust on it, which I like a lot. This is definitely not bland tofu! The color of the green, creamy avocado is great and it makes you feel like you are indulging because it is so buttery. The textures and tastes here send a happy message to your brain. And this is a fast dish to whip up on a weeknight: The tofu is done in five minutes and the avocado sauce gets made in the food processor. *serves 4*

for the tofu: Place a nonstick grill pan over medium-high heat or preheat a gas or charcoal grill.

Cut the tofu in half diagonally to make 2 large triangles. Cut each large triangle in half to make 4 smaller triangles. Cut through each triangle horizontally to make 8 triangles. Brush on each side with the olive oil. Season with the herbes de Provence, salt, and pepper. Grill the tofu until light golden, 2 minutes per side. Transfer to plates.

for the avocado cream: Meanwhile, in a food processor, blend the avocado, olive oil, lime zest, lime juice, broth, parsley, garlic, salt, and pepper until smooth.

Spoon the avocado cream over the tofu and serve.

chicken

Vegetable oil cooking spray

4 (4-ounce) boneless, skinless chicken breast halves

3 tablespoons extra-virgin olive oil

1 teaspoon kosher salt

½ teaspoon freshly ground black pepper

dressing

½ cup extra-virgin olive oil

½ small red onion, roughly chopped

¼ cup fresh lemon juice (from 1 large lemon)

2 tablespoons apple cider vinegar

2 garlic cloves, smashed

½ packed cup fresh basil leaves

¼ packed cup fresh mint leaves

2 tablespoons chopped fresh marjoram leaves

1 tablespoon chopped fresh rosemary leaves

1 tablespoon anchovy paste

1 teaspoon kosher salt

½ teaspoon freshly ground black pepper

per serving: Calories 515; Protein 34g; Carbohydrates 4g; Dietary Fiber 1g; Sugar 1g; Total Fat 40g; Saturated Fat 6g; Sodium 737mg

southern italian-style herbed chicken

The flavors of this chicken come straight from Southern Italy: tons of vibrant fresh herbs, bright lemon juice, some red onion, and a hint of anchovy paste. Don't let the anchovy scare you; it just brings the other flavors to life and makes them taste more like themselves. *serves 4*

for the chicken: Preheat the oven to 425°F.

Spray a heavy rimmed baking sheet with vegetable oil cooking spray. Rub the chicken with the oil and season with the salt and pepper. Arrange the chicken pieces on the baking sheet and roast until cooked through and the internal temperature of the chicken reaches 165°F, about 15 minutes.

for the dressing: While the chicken is roasting, combine the oil, onion, lemon juice, vinegar, garlic, basil, mint, marjoram, rosemary, anchovy paste, salt, and pepper in a food processor. Blend until chunky.

Spoon the dressing on top of the chicken and serve.

¼ cup extra-virgin olive oil

2 large fresh poblano chiles, seeded and diced

1 large onion, chopped

1 celery stalk, chopped

4 large garlic cloves, smashed and chopped

1½ pounds ground dark turkey meat

1 tablespoon all-purpose flour

¼ cup tomato paste

3 tablespoons chili powder

1 tablespoon ground cumin

1 teaspoon dried oregano, crushed

½ teaspoon ground cinnamon

⅛ teaspoon ground cloves

2 packed teaspoons dark brown sugar

1 teaspoon kosher salt

½ teaspoon freshly ground black pepper

3 cups low-sodium chicken broth

1 (15-ounce) can cannellini beans, rinsed and drained

per serving: Calories 419; Protein 28g; Carbohydrates 22g; Dietary Fiber 7g; Sugar 3g; Total Fat 26g; Saturated Fat 6g; Sodium 521mg

california turkey chili

I usually go California style, with bright citrus to enliven my dishes, but here the warming flavors come straight from the Southwest: chili powder, cumin, cinnamon, and clove. To lighten things up, I make my chili with turkey and beans instead of all beef—which I know some people might find controversial. But I have to say I still find myself craving this and, like all good chili, it is even better the next day. Since this dish has such a hearty texture, I like to serve it over light, fluffy quinoa or whole-wheat couscous. Top with chopped onion and tomatoes and shredded white Cheddar cheese, if desired. *Serves 6*

In a heavy large pot or Dutch oven, heat the oil over medium-high heat. Add the poblanos, onion, celery, and garlic. Sauté until the vegetables soften, 5 to 6 minutes.

Add the turkey and sauté, breaking up the turkey with the back of a spoon, until no longer pink, about 7 minutes. Sprinkle the flour over the meat and stir to blend. Add the tomato paste, chili powder, cumin, oregano, cinnamon, cloves, brown sugar, salt, and pepper. Cook, stirring to blend, for 1 to 2 minutes.

Add the broth and beans. Bring to a simmer. Reduce the heat to medium-low and simmer, stirring often, until the flavors blend and the chili thickens, 20 to 30 minutes.

Spoon the chili into deep bowls and serve.

¼ cup extra-virgin olive oil

2 large fresh poblano chiles, seeded; 1 diced, 1 cut into 4 strips

1 (8-ounce) sweet potato, peeled and cut into ⅓-inch cubes

1 (8-ounce) Yukon Gold potato, peeled and cut into ⅓-inch cubes

1 cup chopped onion

4 large tomatillos (8 to 9 ounces total), husked, rinsed, cored, and chopped

4 large garlic cloves, smashed and chopped

1 tablespoon all-purpose flour

2 tablespoons dried oregano

2 teaspoons ground cumin

1 teaspoon kosher salt

½ teaspoon freshly ground black pepper

2 (15-ounce) cans hominy with juices

1 cup vegetable broth

1 (7-ounce) can diced mild green chiles

per serving: Calories 269; Protein 4g; Carbohydrates 40g; Dietary Fiber 8g; Sugar 4g; Total Fat 11g; Saturated Fat 1g; Sodium 629mg

vegetarian chili verde

There are no beans in this recipe; instead, it is loaded with lots of other goodies: Yukon Gold potatoes, sweet potatoes, and my new fave, hominy, which is big bits of puffy corn. You can really sink your teeth into it, so you don't need the beans. This recipe is slightly spicy from mild green chile peppers and very bright from tomatillos. In an effort to replace meat, salt, and fat, I've branched out and discovered new ingredients to keep my cooking interesting. You can go wild with garnishes, such as crumbled feta cheese, chopped scallions, sliced avocado, lime wedges, and, for extra heat, chopped serrano chiles. *serves 6*

In a heavy large pot or Dutch oven, heat the oil over medium heat. Add both of the poblanos, the sweet potato, Yukon Gold potato, onion, tomatillos, and garlic. Cover and cook, stirring often, until the onion is tender, about 8 minutes. Mix in the flour, oregano, cumin, salt, and pepper. Add the hominy with juices and the broth and bring to a simmer.

Spoon the diced green chiles into a food processor. Using tongs, transfer the 4 strips of poblano chile from the pot to the processor. Blend the chiles until just smooth. Scrape the chile sauce into the pot.

Cover and simmer the chili over low heat for 20 minutes. Uncover and simmer, stirring often, until the potatoes are tender and the chili is thickened, 20 to 25 minutes longer. Season to taste with more salt and pepper, if desired.

Ladle the chili into bowls and serve.

per serving: Calories 302; Protein 22g; Carbohydrates 9g; Dietary Fiber 3g; Sugar 4g; Total Fat 20g; Saturated Fat 3g; Sodium 256mg

christmas seafood salad

Despite the name of this recipe, you can make it year-round; it's just a traditional part of an Italian Christmas Eve dinner. Instead of making a pasta with seafood, which is what happens a lot of the time, I lightened it up by turning it into a seafood salad. The seafood is poached and then dressed in classic, simple flavors that complement fish so well: lemon, garlic, rosemary, and olive oil. Just-cooked vegetables—carrots, cauliflower, and green beans—mimic the colors of the Italian flag. I often dress up a platter of this with a ring of beet wedges for their beautiful color (you can use canned or I've included a Cook's Note for how I like to cook them) and serve it with thick slices of toasted country bread for those who want it. *serves 6*

for the dressing: In a medium bowl, whisk together the vinegar, garlic, rosemary, lemon zest, lemon juice, salt, and pepper until blended. Gradually whisk in the oil to emulsify.

for the vegetables: Add enough cold water to a heavy large pot to reach a depth of 2 inches. Bring the water to a boil over medium-high heat and add the salt. Add the carrots, green beans, and cauliflower. Cook until crisp-tender, about 5 minutes. Using a slotted spoon, remove the vegetables and transfer to a bowl to cool. Reserve the water in the pot.

for the seafood: Add the wine to the vegetable cooking water. Adjust the heat so the liquid is barely simmering. Add the cod and simmer until cooked through, about 5 minutes. Using a slotted spoon, remove the cod and set aside on a plate. Add the shrimp and clams to the pot. Cover and cook until all the clams have opened and the shrimp are cooked through and opaque in the center, 4 to 5 minutes. Discard any unopened clams. Drain the shrimp and clams and transfer to the plate with the cod.

to assemble the salad: Arrange the carrots, green beans, and cauliflower on a large platter. Arrange the shrimp, clams, and cod on top and drizzle with the dressing. Arrange the lemon wedges around the edge of the platter and serve.

cook's note

To cook beets, put them in a medium saucepan. Fill the saucepan with water until the beets are covered. Bring to a boil, then lower the heat and cover the pan. Simmer until the beets are cooked through, about 30 minutes. (Alternatively, place the beets in a large microwave-safe bowl. Add 1 cup water. Cover with plastic wrap and cook on high power until tender, about 15 minutes.) Peel the beets under cold running water and cut each into 6 or 8 wedges.

4 (4-ounce) skinless salmon fillets, each about 1 inch thick

¼ cup extra-virgin olive oil

½ teaspoon kosher salt

½ teaspoon freshly ground black pepper

1 tablespoon minced fresh rosemary leaves

4 lemon slices

4 tablespoons lemon juice (from 1 large lemon)

8 tablespoons Marsala wine

4 teaspoons capers, rinsed and drained

per serving: Calories 341; Protein 23g; Carbohydrates 6g; Dietary Fiber 0g; Sugar 4g; Total Fat 21g; Saturated Fat 4g; Sodium 265mg

salmon with lemon, capers, and rosemary

Slip this super-easy dish into your weeknight rotation. Cooking fish in foil seals in all the flavor and keeps the fish extra moist. This recipe also has some bright citrus and briny capers complemented by fragrant rosemary. Salmon takes to these bold flavors really well and this smells just great while it cooks.

serves 4

Place a grill pan over medium-high heat or preheat a gas or charcoal grill.

Put each piece of salmon on a piece of aluminum foil large enough to fold over and seal. Brush the salmon fillets on both sides with olive oil and season with the salt, pepper, and rosemary. Top each piece of salmon with 1 lemon slice, 1 tablespoon lemon juice, 2 tablespoons wine, and 1 teaspoon capers. Wrap the salmon tightly in the foil packets.

Put the foil packets on the hot grill pan or grill rack and cook until medium, about 10 minutes. Transfer the foil packets to plates or shallow bowls and serve, letting everyone open up the foil.

chicken

1 (4½- to 5-pound) chicken, rinsed and patted dry

5 sprigs fresh rosemary, plus 1 teaspoon chopped fresh rosemary leaves

5 sprigs fresh thyme, plus 1 teaspoon chopped fresh thyme leaves

1 lemon, quartered, plus ½ teaspoon lemon juice

2 tablespoons unsalted butter, at room temperature

1 large garlic clove, minced

1 teaspoon kosher salt

½ teaspoon freshly ground black pepper

vegetables

3 tablespoons extra-virgin olive oil

6 baby red potatoes, halved

4 medium carrots, peeled and halved lengthwise

2 large parsnips, peeled and quartered lengthwise

2 large shallots (about 8 ounces), peeled and halved

1 garlic clove, peeled

1 teaspoon chopped fresh rosemary leaves

1 teaspoon chopped fresh thyme leaves

1 teaspoon kosher salt

½ teaspoon freshly ground black pepper

½ cup low-sodium chicken broth

per serving: Calories 520; Protein 33g; Carbohydrates 41g; Dietary Fiber 6g; Sugar 8g; Total Fat 24g; Saturated Fat 7g; Sodium 495mg

garlic-roasted chicken and root vegetables

This is a great recipe to make in fall on the weekend; I like to have leftovers during the week for lunch or to reinvent for dinner. I puree any leftover root veggies in a blender or food processor with a little olive oil, lemon juice, salt, and pepper and turn them into a dressing for a salad. You get a completely new dish (see page 86). *serves 6*

Position an oven rack just below the center of the oven. Preheat the oven to 400°F.

for the chicken: Put the chicken in a large roasting pan and stuff the rosemary sprigs, thyme sprigs, and lemon quarters into the cavity.

In a small bowl, combine the butter, garlic, chopped rosemary, chopped thyme, lemon juice, salt, and pepper until smooth. Smear the butter mixture over the outside and under the skin of the chicken, being careful not to tear the skin.

for the vegetables: In a large bowl, toss together the oil, potatoes, carrots, parsnips, shallots, garlic, rosemary, thyme, salt, and pepper.

Arrange the vegetables around the chicken in a single layer. Pour in the broth. Roast until the vegetables are tender and an instant-read thermometer inserted into the thickest part of the chicken thigh registers 160°F to 165°F, about 1½ hours. Let the chicken rest for 20 minutes.

Transfer the chicken to a platter. Arrange the vegetables around the chicken. Scrape the juices from the roasting pan into a 4-cup measuring cup. Spoon off the layer of fat that rises to the top. Serve the chicken with the pan juices.

in my bag

Sometimes my bag feels like a suitcase, not a handbag! Like most moms, I manage to pack a lot in there so I am always prepared:

- **ALMONDS** for me and, for Jade, **TRAIL MIX** with nuts, raisins, and mini chocolate chips

- A little **DARK CHOCOLATE**; the chocolate-covered espresso beans from the Hôtel de Paris in Monaco are a recent favorite!

- Packets of **AGAVE NECTAR** and **OLIVE OIL**

- **GREEN TEA BAGS**

- **VITAMIN C** packets—an essential for frequent flyers!

- **PROBIOTICS.** When you're eating funny things, at odd times, and have jet lag, these are a must. A lot of the pitfalls of traveling can be prevented by keeping your tummy happy.

- **TIC TACS** or **MINTY GUM** for a quick refreshing fix

- Intensely creamy **HAND CREAM**

- **CRAYONS** for Jade

- Lemon-scented **HAND WIPES**

- Travel-size **PERFUME**, such as tuberose and jasmine

- Travel-size day-to-night **MAKEUP ESSENTIALS**: tinted moisturizer with SPF (great for touchups after work; perks you up), cream shadows (wash hands and use your fingers on eyelids, glowy), lip gloss plus clear gloss with SPF, mascara, cream blush, little mirror with blotters

- **TISSUES**

- **IPHONE** for keeping in touch with photos and Twitter, and for my favorite app, Daily Meditation, which takes just five minutes a day

- **IPAD** with books and games

- **PASHMINA WRAP**: it's my scarf, blanket, and pillow in one!

slaw

2 large oranges

1 grapefruit

1 tablespoon safflower or grapeseed oil

½ tablespoon light agave nectar or honey

½ tablespoon apple cider vinegar

¼ teaspoon bottled horseradish

¼ teaspoon kosher salt

¼ teaspoon freshly ground black pepper

½ small head napa cabbage, finely shredded (3 cups)

pork

Vegetable oil cooking spray

2 teaspoons ground cumin

⅛ teaspoon cayenne pepper

½ teaspoon kosher salt

1 (1-pound) pork tenderloin

1 tablespoon safflower or grapeseed oil

5 baked tortilla chips, crushed

per serving: Calories 326; Protein 26g; Carbohydrates 28g; Dietary Fiber 7g; Sugar 16g; Total Fat 13g; Saturated Fat 3g; Sodium 316mg

sliced pork tenderloin with citrus slaw

This is my much lighter version of a pulled pork taco. I opt for tenderloin instead of pork shoulder, which is fatty and takes a long time to cook. This still has the citrusy flavors and crunchy slaw, but instead of serving it all in a tortilla, I take a few baked tortilla chips and sprinkle them over the top. *serves* 4

for the slaw: Cut the ends off one of the oranges and then use the knife to slice off all of the peel and white pith underneath. Using a paring knife, and holding the orange in your hand, slice between the membranes to release the segments. Cut the segments into ½-inch pieces and put into a bowl. Squeeze the juice from the membranes and reserve. Repeat with the remaining orange and the grapefruit.

In a large bowl, whisk together the oil, 1 tablespoon of the reserved citrus juice, the agave, vinegar, horseradish, salt, and pepper. Add the citrus segments and cabbage. Toss until coated. Refrigerate for 30 minutes.

for the pork: Position an oven rack in the center of the oven and preheat the oven to 400°F. Spray a heavy rimmed baking sheet with vegetable oil cooking spray.

In a small bowl, mix together the cumin, cayenne pepper, and salt. Rub the spice mixture all over the pork. In a large skillet, heat the oil over medium-high heat. Add the pork and brown on all sides, about 8 minutes. Transfer the pork to the prepared baking sheet and bake until a meat thermometer inserted into the thickest part of the meat registers 160°F, about 30 minutes. Allow the meat to rest for 10 minutes before slicing into ¼- to ½-inch-thick slices.

Divide the slaw among 4 plates. Arrange the sliced pork on top and sprinkle with the crushed tortilla chips.

2¾ cups vegetable broth

2 (¼-inch-thick) slices fresh ginger, plus 1 tablespoon plus 1½ teaspoons minced peeled fresh ginger

½ cup wild rice

½ cup short-grain or long-grain brown rice

3 tablespoons safflower or grapeseed oil

1 medium onion, finely chopped (1¼ cups)

3 small carrots, peeled and cut into ⅓-inch cubes (1 cup)

3 garlic cloves, minced

½ cup golden raisins

6 ounces extra-firm tofu, drained, patted dry, and cut into ½-inch cubes

2 teaspoons mild curry powder

1 teaspoon ground cumin

1 small bunch of scallions, white and light green parts, sliced (1 cup), plus more for garnish if desired

½ cup canned coconut milk

½ teaspoon kosher salt

¼ teaspoon freshly ground black pepper

6 large Swiss chard leaves

1 (24-ounce) jar spicy red pepper tomato sauce

per serving: Calories 357; Protein 11g; Carbohydrates 52g; Dietary Fiber 8g; Sugar 15g; Total Fat 14g; Saturated Fat 5g; Sodium 704mg

swiss chard rolls with wild and brown rice and indian spices

This is so yummy! I created this dish because I was catering a charity dinner with Alice Waters, Nancy Silverton, and Suzanne Goin for Alex's Lemonade Stand and we needed a vegan dish. Rather than just taking cheese out of a pasta dish, I wanted to dream up a whole new recipe. This is loaded with flavor and gorgeous to look at. It's creamy, spicy, sweet, and just as good as anything loaded with cheese. *serves 6*

In a medium saucepan, combine the vegetable broth and sliced ginger. Bring to a boil. Add wild and brown rices, and return to a boil. Reduce the heat to medium-low, cover, and simmer until the rice is just tender, 50 to 55 minutes (the wild rice will still have a slight bite). Drain if necessary. Discard the ginger slices.

Meanwhile, position the oven rack in the center of the oven and preheat the oven to 400°F. Lightly oil a 9 x 13-inch glass baking dish with 1 tablespoon of the oil.

Bring a large pot of salted water to a boil.

Heat the remaining 2 tablespoons oil in a large nonstick skillet over medium-high heat. Add the onion and carrots to the skillet and cook, stirring often, until the vegetables are tender and the onion is golden, 6 to 7 minutes. Add the garlic and minced ginger and stir for 1 minute.

Add the raisins, tofu cubes, 1½ teaspoons of the curry powder, and the cumin and stir gently to coat the tofu with the spices. Mix in the scallions. Pour in the coconut milk and simmer just until the

RECIPE CONTINUES

coconut milk is reduced and coats the vegetable mixture thickly, about 1 minute. Stir in the rice mixture and season with the salt and pepper. Remove from the heat and let cool while preparing the chard leaves.

Using a sharp knife, cut away and discard the thick stems from the center of each Swiss chard leaf. Cut each leaf in half lengthwise. Trim the wide ends from the leaves to make each leaf half about 10 inches long. Using tongs and working with 1 leaf half at a time, dip the leaf half into the pot of boiling salted water for 10 seconds and then transfer to paper towels to drain.

Put 1 Swiss chard leaf half on a cutting board. Spoon ⅓ packed cup of the rice filling onto one end of the leaf. Fold the sides of the leaf up over the filling, then roll up the leaf, enclosing the filling completely (like a burrito). Repeat with the remaining leaf halves and rice filling for a total of 12 rolls.

Mix the remaining ½ teaspoon curry powder into the tomato sauce. Spread 1 cup of the sauce onto the bottom of the prepared baking dish. Arrange the filled rolls, seam side down, in a single layer atop the sauce in the dish. Spoon the remaining tomato sauce over the rolls. Bake until the rolls are heated through, 25 to 30 minutes. Garnish with sliced scallions, if desired, and serve.

sauce

1 tablespoon extra-virgin olive oil

⅛ teaspoon crushed red pepper flakes

2 garlic cloves, finely chopped

1 (12-ounce) jar roasted red bell peppers, rinsed, drained, and chopped

1 (14.5-ounce) can crushed tomatoes with juice

1 tablespoon tomato paste

1 teaspoon light agave nectar

¼ cup chopped fresh basil leaves

¼ teaspoon kosher salt

fish

4 (4-ounce) pieces skinless striped bass fillets, about 1 inch thick

1 teaspoon kosher salt

½ teaspoon freshly ground black pepper

1 tablespoon extra-virgin olive oil

per serving: Calories 256; Protein 23g; Carbohydrates 15g; Dietary Fiber 3g; Sugar 2g; Total Fat 10g; Saturated Fat 2g; Sodium 785mg

grilled striped bass with tomato and bell pepper sauce

This flavorful tomato–bell pepper sauce can top anything—fish, steak, shrimp, pasta, vegetables, and more. I often make a double batch and keep it on hand to use throughout the week. The fennel in it brings me back to my Italian roots; I love that light anise flavor, especially with fish. It's a classic Southern Italian pairing. *Serves 4*

for the sauce: In a medium saucepan, heat the oil over medium heat. Add the red pepper flakes and cook until fragrant, 1 to 2 minutes. Add the garlic and cook for 30 seconds. Add the bell peppers, tomatoes with their juices, tomato paste, and agave. Bring to a simmer, whisking to blend. Reduce the heat to low and simmer until slightly thickened, about 10 minutes. Stir in the basil and salt.

for the fish: Preheat a grill pan over medium-high heat.

Season the fish on both sides with salt and pepper. Drizzle the fish with the olive oil. Grill the fish until cooked through and the flesh flakes easily with a fork, 4 to 5 minutes per side.

Transfer the fish to 4 plates and spoon the sauce on top.

First things first: I have curly hair, so I always brush it in the shower. And I am absolutely hopeless with a blow dryer! I have no patience to do it right, so I get a professional blow-out once a week and then muddle through as best as I can for the rest of the week. I stay away from flat irons, which can break my hair, especially around my face. At night, I wear a high ponytail to bed so I can hold on to the styling from the day before.

I do color my hair. On camera grays really stand out so I like to cover them. I alternate between covering the grays at the roots and getting highlights every six to eight weeks. The longer I can go, the better for my hair.

After traveling or filming for television under hot lights, both of which really dry out my hair, I use this natural beauty treatment to restore its shine: In the shower—with plenty of steam—I rub a half cup of olive oil (not expensive extra-virgin olive oil, just regular olive oil) into my scalp. I leave it in for up to ten minutes with a shower cap on while I take my shower or shave my legs. Then I shampoo it out; sometimes I need two shampoos to remove it.

If you have a dry scalp and use a lot of products, especially if you use dry shampoo, you can try this: Mix one small avocado with a quarter to a half cup of olive oil. Blend together until smooth and then massage into your hair and scalp. Leave it in for ten to twenty minutes and then shampoo.

Natural Instincts also makes an amazing deep conditioner with coconut oil that I use once a week, alternating with my olive oil routine.

- ¼ cup plus 1 tablespoon extra-virgin olive oil
- 2 tablespoons fresh lemon juice (from 1 large lemon)
- 2 large garlic cloves, smashed
- ¼ teaspoon kosher salt
- ¼ teaspoon freshly ground black pepper
- 8 (2-ounce) skinless sole fillets
- ½ cup Lemon-Basil Pesto (recipe follows)

per serving (includes pesto): Calories 325; Protein 23g; Carbohydrates 3g; Dietary Fiber 1g; Sugar 1g; Total Fat 25g; Saturated Fat 4g; Sodium 287mg

sole with lemon-basil pesto

This no-cook sauce—a particularly bright, citrusy pesto—started as a dipping sauce in my house. But I liked it so much I started making it to serve with sole, which proved to be a great way to get Jade to eat fish. The sole is nice and light and needs only a smear of the lemon-basil pesto to make a simple, elegant dish.
serves 4

In an 8-inch square glass dish, combine ¼ cup of the olive oil, the lemon juice, garlic, salt, and pepper. Whisk the marinade to blend. Add the sole and turn several times to coat evenly. Let stand for 15 minutes.

Heat a large nonstick skillet over medium-high heat. Add the remaining 1 tablespoon olive oil. Remove 4 sole fillets from the marinade, letting any excess marinade drip off, and add to the hot pan. Sear for 2 minutes and then turn the fish over. Sear until just cooked through, about 3 minutes longer. Transfer to plates and repeat with the remaining 4 pieces of sole. Top each serving of sole with 2 tablespoons of the lemon-basil pesto and serve.

RECIPE CONTINUES

lemon-basil pesto

Leftovers can be tossed with whole-wheat pasta or served with fish, meat—or pretty much anything. You can store the pesto, covered and refrigerated, for a couple of days.

MAKES ABOUT ¾ CUP

2 packed cups fresh basil leaves

⅓ cup pine nuts, toasted (see Cook's Note)

Grated zest of 1 large lemon

2 tablespoons fresh lemon juice (from 1 large lemon)

1 garlic clove, smashed and peeled

½ teaspoon kosher salt

¼ teaspoon freshly ground black pepper

⅓ cup extra-virgin olive oil

⅓ cup freshly grated Parmesan cheese

In a blender or food processor, pulse the basil, pine nuts, lemon zest, lemon juice, garlic, salt, and pepper until finely chopped. With the machine running, gradually add the oil and blend until the mixture is smooth and thick. Add the cheese and pulse until just incorporated.

cook's note

To toast pine nuts, arrange in a single layer on a rimmed baking sheet. Bake in a preheated 350°F oven until golden, about 6 minutes. Let cool completely before using.

pork

Vegetable oil cooking spray

1 (1-pound) pork tenderloin

½ teaspoon kosher salt

½ teaspoon freshly ground black pepper

1 tablespoon safflower or grapeseed oil

sauce

1 tablespoon safflower or grapeseed oil

1 large shallot, chopped

¼ teaspoon kosher salt

⅛ teaspoon freshly ground black pepper

1 garlic clove, minced

¼ cup dry white wine, such as pinot grigio

¼ cup honey

¼ cup Dijon mustard

1 tablespoon red wine vinegar

½ tablespoon chopped fresh thyme leaves

2 teaspoons unsalted butter, at room temperature

per serving: Calories 317; Protein 23g; Carbohydrates 20g; Dietary Fiber 0g; Sugar 17g; Total Fat 14g; Saturated Fat 4g; Sodium 618mg

pork tenderloin with honey-mustard sauce

I love honey-mustard anything. The sauce is sweet but it also has a kick. Pork tenderloin cooks quickly and benefits from the added bold flavors from this simple pan sauce, which comes together in minutes while the pork rests. Leftovers make great sandwiches. *Serves 4*

for the pork: Position an oven rack in the center of the oven and preheat the oven to 400°F. Spray a heavy rimmed baking sheet with vegetable oil cooking spray.

Season the pork with the salt and pepper. In a large skillet, heat the oil over medium-high heat. Add the pork and brown on all sides, about 8 minutes. Transfer the pork to the prepared baking sheet and bake until a meat thermometer inserted into the thickest part of the meat registers 160°F, about 30 minutes. Allow the meat to rest for 10 minutes on a cutting board before slicing ¼- to ½-inch-thick slices.

for the sauce: Meanwhile, in the same skillet used for browning the pork, heat the oil over medium-high heat. Add the shallot, salt, and pepper. Cook until soft, about 3 minutes. Add the garlic and cook for 30 seconds. Pour in the wine and use a wooden spoon to scrape up the brown bits that cling to the bottom of the pan. Simmer for 1 minute. Whisk in the honey, mustard, vinegar, and thyme. Simmer until thickened, about 2 minutes. Remove from the heat and stir in the butter until melted and smooth.

Top the pork slices with the honey-mustard sauce and serve.

burgers

½ cup extra-virgin olive oil

2 large shallots, minced

1½ teaspoons kosher salt

½ teaspoon freshly ground black pepper

2 garlic cloves, minced

4 ounces button mushrooms (about 6), finely diced

2 tablespoons chopped fresh thyme leaves

½ cup frozen petite green peas, thawed

2 (15-ounce) cans lentils, rinsed and drained

½ cup plus ⅓ cup cornmeal

2 tablespoons egg-free mayonnaise, such as Vegenaise

1 tablespoon fresh lemon juice

mayonnaise

1 cup refrigerated egg-free mayonnaise, such as Vegenaise

½ cup chopped fresh basil leaves

Grated zest of 1 large lemon

1 head butter lettuce, leaves separated

2 plum tomatoes, thinly sliced

per serving: Calories 584; Protein 7g; Carbohydrates 31g; Dietary Fiber 7g; Sugar 4g; Total Fat 47g; Saturated Fat 6g; Sodium 576mg

lentil burgers with lemon-basil mayonnaise

I make these vegan burgers when I want to eat a bit lighter but crave something that feels indulgent and hearty. They are also great for barbecues, of course. I'm finding more and more that my friends, even those who are meat-eaters, sometimes want a different option. I skip the bread and keep the traditional lettuce and tomato garnishes—and often a pickle, too—but it goes without saying that these are also great on buns. To make mini burgers, see the Cook's Note. *Serves 6*

for the burgers: In a 12-inch nonstick skillet, heat ¼ cup of the oil over medium-high heat. Add the shallots, ¾ teaspoon of the salt, and ¼ teaspoon of the pepper. Cook until soft, about 3 minutes. Add the garlic, mushrooms, thyme, the remaining ¾ teaspoon salt, and the remaining ¼ teaspoon pepper. Cook until the mushrooms are soft, 6 to 8 minutes. Set aside to cool slightly.

In a food processor, puree the peas and half of the lentils until smooth. Transfer to a medium bowl. Add the remaining lentils, ⅓ cup of the cornmeal, the mayonnaise, lemon juice, and the mushroom mixture. Form the mixture into 6 (3-inch-thick) patties.

Sprinkle ¼ cup of the remaining cornmeal on a baking sheet. Put the formed patties on top of the cornmeal. Sprinkle the remaining ¼ cup cornmeal on top of the patties. Refrigerate for at least 30 minutes.

Heat the remaining ¼ cup olive oil in the same skillet over medium heat. Add the patties and cook until they are golden brown, 4 minutes per side.

cook's note

For mini burgers, form the mixture into 12 (2-inch-thick) patties. For sprinkling on the baking sheet and over the burgers, you'll need just ¼ cup cornmeal (instead of ½ cup).

for the mayonnaise: In a small bowl, mix together the mayonnaise, basil, and lemon zest until smooth.

Smear the mayonnaise on the lentil burgers. Serve over the lettuce and tomato slices.

sauce

1 cup finely chopped arugula

⅔ cup finely chopped fresh flat-leaf parsley leaves

½ cup extra-virgin olive oil

¼ cup capers, rinsed and drained

1 teaspoon grated lemon zest

2 tablespoons fresh lemon juice (from 1 large lemon)

¾ teaspoon kosher salt

¼ teaspoon crushed red pepper flakes

fish

2 tablespoons chopped fresh flat-leaf parsley leaves

2 tablespoons chopped fresh chives

1 teaspoon grated lemon zest

4 (4-ounce) skinless salmon fillets, each about 1 inch thick

1 tablespoon extra-virgin olive oil

1 teaspoon kosher salt

¾ teaspoon freshly ground black pepper

Lemon wedges, for serving (optional)

per serving: Calories 478; Protein 27g; Carbohydrates 2g; Dietary Fiber 1g; Sugar 0g; Total Fat 40g; Saturated Fat 6g; Sodium 761mg

baked salmon with arugula salsa verde

A traditional Italian green sauce gets even greener and more vibrant with the addition of chopped arugula; it's kind of like a salad and sauce in one. This dish is great over quinoa or brown rice. *serves* 4

for the sauce: In a small bowl, blend the arugula, parsley, olive oil, capers, lemon zest, lemon juice, salt, and red pepper flakes.

for the fish: Position an oven rack in the center of the oven. Preheat the oven to 375°F.

In a small bowl, mix the parsley, chives, and lemon zest.

Coat the salmon fillets all over with the olive oil. Put the fish on a rimmed baking sheet. Sprinkle on both sides with the salt and pepper. Sprinkle the herb mixture over the top of the fish fillets, pressing slightly to adhere.

Bake the fish until medium, 9 to 10 minutes. Transfer 1 fish fillet to each of 4 plates. Spoon the arugula salsa verde alongside. Serve with lemon wedges, if desired.

tzatziki

1 cup plain low-fat (2%) Greek yogurt

⅓ cup chopped fresh basil leaves

¼ cup chopped fresh chives

2 tablespoons chopped fresh tarragon leaves

1 tablespoon white wine vinegar

¼ teaspoon kosher salt

¼ teaspoon freshly ground black pepper

½ large hothouse cucumber, halved lengthwise and seeded

salmon

3 tablespoons extra-virgin olive oil

4 (4-ounce) skinless salmon fillets, each about 1 inch thick

½ teaspoon kosher salt

¼ teaspoon freshly ground black pepper

per serving: Calories 324; Protein 30g; Carbohydrates 4g; Dietary Fiber 1g; Sugar 3g; Total Fat 20g; Saturated Fat 4g; Sodium 297mg

salmon with basil and chive tzatziki

Salmon pairs so well with the fresh herbs and tangy Greek yogurt in this creamy yet light sauce. This dish feels decadent when you eat it, but it's so good for you! *serves* 4

for the tzatziki: In a food processor, combine the yogurt, basil, chives, tarragon, vinegar, salt, and pepper. Blend until the herbs are finely chopped and the sauce is pale green. Scrape the sauce into a bowl.

Stack 2 paper towels on a plate. Using the large holes of a box grater, coarsely grate the cucumber onto the paper towels; pat dry. Mix the cucumber into the tzatziki sauce. Cover and refrigerate for up to 4 hours. Stir before serving.

for the salmon: In a large skillet, heat the olive oil over medium-high heat. Season the salmon on both sides with the salt and pepper. Put the salmon in the pan, skinned side up, and cook until golden brown, about 4 minutes. Using a fish spatula, flip the fish and cook until medium in the center, about 2 minutes.

Serve the fish warm, at room temperature, or chilled, topped with the tzatziki.

sauce

1 medium mango, peeled, seeded, and cut into ½-inch pieces, or 1¼ cups frozen mango pieces, thawed

½ cup fresh orange juice

1 (2-inch) piece of fresh ginger, peeled and minced

¼ teaspoon kosher salt

⅛ teaspoon freshly ground black pepper

1 vanilla bean, preferably Tahitian

2 tablespoons unsalted butter, at room temperature

fish

1 tablespoon extra-virgin olive oil

4 (4-ounce) skinless mahimahi or halibut fillets, each 1 inch thick

1 teaspoon kosher salt

½ teaspoon freshly ground black pepper

per serving: Calories 358; Protein 18g; Carbohydrates 12g; Dietary Fiber 1g; Sugar 11g; Total Fat 26g; Saturated Fat 7g; Sodium 450mg

mahimahi with mango-vanilla sauce

 gf

This recipe is inspired by my trip to Bora Bora, where I ate many mahimahi dishes. The mango sauce isn't overly sweet because it is balanced with bright orange juice and spicy ginger. What makes this dish is the vanilla bean. The little flecks of seeds add such wonderful aroma and flavor. When I make this, it takes me back to the tropics and I feel like I am still on vacation! *serves 4*

for the sauce: In a blender, combine the mango, orange juice, ¼ cup water, the ginger, salt, and pepper. Blend until smooth and then pour into a small saucepan. Using a paring knife, cut the vanilla bean in half lengthwise and scrape the seeds into the saucepan. Add the empty vanilla pod halves, too. Bring the mixture to a boil over medium-high heat. Reduce the heat and simmer for 6 minutes. Remove the vanilla pod halves and discard. Remove the pan from the heat and whisk in the butter until smooth.

for the fish: In a 12-inch nonstick skillet, heat the oil over medium-high heat. Season the fish on both sides with the salt and pepper. Add the fish to the pan and cook until the fish flakes easily with a fork, 6 to 8 minutes per side.

Arrange the fish on plates and spoon the sauce on top.

vegetables

Vegetable oil cooking spray

1 small (1-pound) butternut squash, peeled, seeded, and cut into ½-inch dice (3 cups)

2 medium zucchini, cut into ½-inch pieces

1 red bell pepper, cut into ½-inch pieces

1 (15-ounce) can kidney beans, rinsed and drained

3 tablespoons extra-virgin olive oil

2 teaspoons ground cumin

1½ teaspoons dried oregano

1 teaspoon kosher salt

2 whole-wheat pita breads

chipotle cream

1 small canned chipotle pepper, finely diced

½ cup plain nonfat (0%) Greek yogurt

1 tablespoon fresh lime juice

1 teaspoon light agave nectar

per serving: Calories 344; Protein 13g; Carbohydrates 51g; Dietary Fiber 14g; Sugar 8g; Total Fat 2g; Saturated Fat 2g; Sodium 604mg

roasted vegetables with chipotle cream over crispy pita

This recipe takes all the great flavors of a Mexican tostada and turns them into a lighter dish. I replace the fried tostada with crispy whole-wheat pita and use nonfat Greek yogurt to make the chipotle sauce. You still get the crunch and the creaminess of the original, but you don't need to take a siesta after you eat this!

serves 4

Position an oven rack in the center of the oven and preheat the oven to 425°F.

for the vegetables: Spray a heavy rimmed baking sheet with vegetable oil cooking spray. In a medium bowl, toss together the butternut squash, zucchini, bell pepper, kidney beans, oil, cumin, oregano, and salt. Spread the mixture in a single layer on the baking sheet. Roast until the vegetables are golden and tender, 25 to 30 minutes.

Split the pita breads in half horizontally to make 4 rounds. Arrange in a single layer on a heavy baking sheet. Bake until crisp, 7 to 8 minutes. Set aside to cool.

for the chipotle cream: In a small bowl, mix together the chipotle pepper, yogurt, lime juice, and agave until smooth.

Spread a dollop of the chipotle cream over each crispy pita and spoon the vegetable mixture on top.

cook's note

For a milder chipotle sauce, remove the seeds in the chipotle pepper before adding to the sauce.

fish

Vegetable oil cooking spray

8 (2-ounce) skinless sole fish fillets

½ teaspoon kosher salt

½ teaspoon freshly ground black pepper

2 tablespoons extra-virgin olive oil

sauce

⅓ cup plain low-fat (2%) Greek yogurt

½ teaspoon light agave nectar or honey

½ teaspoon Dijon mustard

2 tablespoons fresh lemon juice (from 1 large lemon)

2 tablespoons chopped fresh chives

¼ teaspoon kosher salt

¼ teaspoon freshly ground black pepper

per serving: Calories 214; Protein 29g; Carbohydrates 2g; Dietary Fiber 0g; Sugar 2g; Total Fat 9g; Saturated Fat 2g; Sodium 354mg

broiled sole with mustard-chive sauce

I make this at least once every other week—it's that simple; I know the proportions by heart at this point! Any mild-flavored white fish works well here. Serve with brown rice and a green vegetable; broccoli or a simple salad would be nice. *serves 4*

for the fish: Preheat the broiler.

Spray a heavy rimmed baking sheet or glass baking dish with vegetable oil cooking spray. Arrange the sole fillets in a single layer on the baking sheet. Season with the salt and pepper and drizzle with the olive oil. Broil until cooked through and the flesh flakes easily with a fork, 5 to 6 minutes. Set aside to cool slightly.

for the sauce: Meanwhile, in a small bowl, mix together the yogurt, agave, and mustard until smooth. Whisk in the lemon juice, chives, salt, and pepper.

Transfer the sole to a serving platter and drizzle with the sauce.

chicken

1 cup plain low-fat (2%) Greek yogurt

2 tablespoons frozen apple juice concentrate, thawed

1 tablespoon apple cider vinegar

2 teaspoons garam masala

1 teaspoon kosher salt

1 teaspoon freshly ground black pepper

8 (2-ounce) skinless chicken cutlets, each about ¼ inch thick

chutney

3 tablespoons apple cider vinegar

2 tablespoons apricot preserves

1 small red jalapeño chile, seeded, deveined, and finely chopped

2 tablespoons Dijon mustard

1 teaspoon hot sauce, such as Cholula (optional)

½ teaspoon kosher salt

½ teaspoon freshly ground black pepper

⅛ teaspoon ground cloves

⅛ teaspoon ground ginger

1 apple, such as Gala, cut into ⅓-inch dice (about 1¼ cups)

1 small mango, peeled and cut into ⅓-inch dice (about 1 cup)

¼ cup chopped fresh mint leaves, plus some sprigs for garnish

Vegetable oil cooking spray

per serving: Calories 252; Protein 27g; Carbohydrates 26g; Dietary Fiber 2g; Sugar 23g; Total Fat 4g; Saturated Fat 2g; Sodium 620mg

grilled chicken cutlets with fresh apple-mango chutney

This chicken alone is so good—even as leftovers, straight from the fridge! The marinade, a twist on Indian tandoori preparation, keeps the chicken super-moist and then makes an amazing savory crust on it that's completely addictive. The fresh chutney is crunchy and refreshing while still holding on to the classic sweet-tart flavors. *Serves* 4

for the chicken: In a glass baking dish, whisk together the yogurt, apple juice concentrate, vinegar, garam masala, salt, and pepper until combined. Add the chicken and turn to coat. Cover and marinate in the refrigerator for at least 2 hours or up to 1 day.

for the chutney: In a medium bowl, stir together the vinegar, apricot preserves, jalapeño, mustard, hot sauce, salt, pepper, cloves, and ginger until blended. Mix in the apple, mango, and chopped mint. Let stand for up to 30 minutes before serving, or cover and refrigerate for up to 2 days.

Place a grill pan over medium-high heat or preheat a gas or charcoal grill. Spray the grill lightly with vegetable oil cooking spray.

Put the chicken cutlets (still coated with marinade) on the grill. Grill until cooked through, 4 to 5 minutes per side. Transfer the chicken to plates, serving 2 pieces per person, and let rest for 5 minutes.

Spoon some chutney alongside the chicken. Garnish with mint sprigs and serve.

peppers

6 large red bell peppers

½ cup whole-wheat couscous

1 teaspoon kosher salt

Vegetable oil cooking spray

1 tablespoon extra-virgin olive oil

1 large shallot, diced (about ½ cup)

3 large garlic cloves, chopped

1½ teaspoons dried oregano

½ teaspoon freshly ground black pepper

⅓ cup raisins

¼ cup slivered almonds, coarsely chopped

10 pitted kalamata olives, chopped

1 tablespoon fresh lime juice (2 to 3 large limes)

3 tablespoons pure maple syrup

4 ounces coarsely grated low-fat white Cheddar cheese (1 cup)

avocado sauce

1 (12-ounce) avocado, chopped

2 tablespoons fresh lime juice (from 2 large limes)

½ teaspoon kosher salt

per serving: Calories 365; Protein 11g; Carbohydrates 46g; Dietary Fiber 10g; Sugar 18g; Total Fat 17g; Saturated Fat 4g; Sodium 518mg

stuffed red bell peppers with whole-wheat couscous and avocado sauce

This is a great make-ahead vegetarian dish. Stuff the peppers, store them in the fridge, and then pop the dish in the oven half an hour before dinner. And it's anything but bland; it has bright notes from salty olives, crunchy almonds, plump sweet raisins, and gooey cheese. *serves 6*

for the peppers: Preheat a broiler.

Arrange the peppers in a single layer on a heavy rimmed baking sheet. Broil, turning the peppers every few minutes, until charred on all sides, 5 to 10 minutes. Put the peppers in a resealable plastic bag for 15 minutes. Gently scrape off the burnt skin, being careful not to tear the flesh. Lay each pepper on a cutting board. Using a paring knife, remove a ½-inch-wide strip of flesh from the side of each pepper to create an opening. Chop the strips of pepper into ½-inch pieces to reserve for the filling. Using a small spoon, remove the seeds from inside each pepper.

In a medium saucepan, bring ¾ cup water to a boil over medium-high heat. Stir in the couscous and ½ teaspoon of the salt. Simmer for 1 minute. Remove the pan from the heat and cover. Let stand for 5 minutes. Uncover and fluff the couscous with a fork.

Position a rack in the center of the oven and preheat the oven to 400°F. Spray a 9 x 13-inch baking dish with vegetable oil cooking spray.

In a small nonstick skillet, heat the oil over medium-high heat. Add the shallot, garlic, oregano, the remaining ½ teaspoon salt, and the pepper. Cook until the shallots are soft, about 3 minutes.

In a large bowl, combine the couscous, shallot mixture, the reserved chopped bell pepper pieces, the raisins, almonds, olives, lime juice, maple syrup, and half of the cheese.

Divide the filling among the peppers, packing it gently and mounding it at the top. Arrange in the prepared dish, spaced slightly apart. Sprinkle the remaining cheese on top and bake until the peppers are heated through, 10 to 15 minutes.

for the avocado sauce: Meanwhile, in a food processor, combine the avocado, 2 tablespoons water, the lime juice, and salt. Blend for 2 minutes, scraping down the sides of the bowl as needed, until the mixture is smooth.

Spoon the sauce on plates and top with the peppers.

1 pound whole-wheat
   linguine

2 tablespoons extra-virgin
   olive oil

3 large garlic cloves,
   chopped

½ teaspoon crushed red
   pepper flakes

2 pints cherry tomatoes,
   stemmed and halved

½ cup dry white wine, such
   as pinot grigio

1 pound asparagus, stalks
   cut on the diagonal into
   1- to 1½-inch pieces

1 pound large shrimp, peeled
   and deveined

½ cup chopped fresh mint
   leaves

½ cup chopped fresh basil
   leaves

2 teaspoons chopped fresh
   oregano leaves

½ teaspoon kosher salt

¾ teaspoon freshly ground
   black pepper

per serving: Calories 427;
Protein 24g; Carbohydrates
65g; Dietary Fiber 11g;
Sugar 4g; Total Fat 6g;
Saturated Fat 1g; Sodium
248mg

whole-wheat linguine with shrimp, asparagus, and cherry tomatoes

This colorful, beautiful summery dish feeds a small crowd. It is one of those impressive, company-is-coming-over dishes that still comes together quickly on a weeknight. *serves 6*

Bring a large pot of salted water to a boil over high heat. Add the pasta and cook, stirring occasionally, until tender but still firm to the bite, 8 to 10 minutes. Drain and transfer to a large bowl.

Meanwhile, in a large, deep skillet, heat the oil over medium-high heat. Add the garlic and red pepper flakes. Stir until aromatic, 30 seconds. Add the tomatoes and cook, stirring occasionally, until they soften, about 2 minutes. Using a fork, lightly mash the tomatoes. Add the wine and asparagus. Bring to a boil, lower the heat, and simmer for 5 minutes. Add the shrimp and continue to simmer until the shrimp are cooked through, 5 to 7 minutes. Stir in the mint, basil, oregano, salt, and pepper.

Pour the sauce over the pasta and toss to combine. Serve immediately.

chicken

¼ cup extra-virgin olive oil

Grated zest of 1 large lemon

¼ cup fresh lemon juice (from 1 large lemon)

2 garlic cloves, minced

1 tablespoon ground cumin

1 teaspoon kosher salt

¼ teaspoon crushed red pepper flakes

4 (4-ounce) boneless, skinless chicken breast halves

pesto

1½ packed cups fresh mint leaves

1 packed cup baby spinach leaves

½ cup freshly grated Parmesan cheese

⅓ cup walnut pieces, toasted (see Cook's Note, page 89)

1 garlic clove, smashed and peeled

2 teaspoons fresh lemon juice (from 1 large lemon)

½ teaspoon kosher salt

½ teaspoon freshly ground black pepper

½ cup extra-virgin olive oil

Vegetable oil cooking spray

per serving: Calories 240; Protein 27g; Carbohydrates 2g; Dietary Fiber 1g; Sugar 1g; Total Fat 13g; Saturated Fat 4g; Sodium 395mg

lemon-cumin chicken with mint and spinach pesto

What makes this pesto different is that I use walnuts instead of pine nuts and spinach and mint in place of parsley or basil. This recipe makes eating raw spinach exciting—and, trust me, I'm not a raw-spinach-salad kind of person! But I really enjoy it this way. The mint sweetens it and the salty, savory Parmesan seals the deal. Cumin gives a citrusy spice to the chicken, which pairs so well with these flavors. *serves 4*

for the chicken: In a glass baking dish, whisk together the oil, lemon zest, lemon juice, garlic, cumin, salt, and pepper flakes until smooth. Add the chicken and turn to coat with the marinade. Cover and refrigerate for at least 4 hours or overnight.

for the pesto: In a food processor, blend the mint, spinach, cheese, walnuts, garlic, lemon juice, salt, and pepper until chunky. With the machine running, slowly add the olive oil and process until smooth.

Place a grill pan over medium-high heat or preheat a gas or charcoal grill. Spray the grill lightly with vegetable oil cooking spray.

Remove the chicken from the marinade. Discard the marinade. Grill the chicken until cooked through, 4 to 5 minutes per side.

Transfer the chicken to plates and serve with the pesto.

dessert

½ cup bittersweet chocolate chips, such as Ghirardelli

4 very ripe large avocados, chopped

½ cup unsweetened cocoa powder

½ cup light agave nectar

1 tablespoon plus 1 teaspoon pure vanilla extract

¼ teaspoon fine sea salt

⅓ cup unsweetened almond milk

Fresh raspberries, for garnish

per serving: Calories 326; Protein 4g; Carbohydrates 42g; Dietary Fiber 7g; Sugar 22g; Total Fat 19g; Saturated Fat 5g; Sodium 105mg

avocado-chocolate mousse with raspberries

I know what you're thinking, that this is going to taste like avocado; but the chocolate is what comes through, actually. This is a great substitute for a traditional mousse; you get the same texture without dairy. Make sure the avocadoes are ripe so you get a smooth—and not lumpy—mousse. *Serves 6*

Put the chocolate chips in a heat-proof medium bowl. Set over a small saucepan of barely simmering water. Stir until the chocolate is melted and smooth, about 3 minutes. Set aside to cool slightly.

In a food processor, combine the melted chocolate, the avocados, cocoa powder, agave, vanilla, salt, and almond milk. Blend until smooth and creamy, scraping the sides of the bowl as needed. Spoon into glasses and refrigerate for at least 3 hours or up to 1 day.

Garnish with raspberries before serving.

filling

1 pound frozen peaches, thawed, or 3 large peaches, pitted and thinly sliced

1 pound frozen blueberries, thawed and drained, or 1½ cups fresh blueberries

2 tablespoons pure maple syrup

2 teaspoons pure vanilla extract

1½ teaspoons ground cinnamon

Grated zest of 1 large lemon

2 tablespoons fresh lemon juice (from 1 large lemon)

¼ teaspoon fine sea salt

topping

¾ cup sliced almonds

½ cup old-fashioned rolled oats

2 tablespoons honey

1 tablespoon safflower or grapeseed oil

½ teaspoon ground cinnamon

per serving: Calories 162; Protein 3g; Carbohydrates 24g; Dietary Fiber 4g; Sugar 16g; Total Fat 7g; Saturated Fat 1g; Sodium 63mg

peach and blueberry crumble

This is a new take on a quintessential all-American dessert. All my favorite things about a great crumble are here: the tartness of the blueberries, the sweet syrup of the baked peaches, and the crunchy, crust-like topping—but without all the sugar you will normally find hanging out in this dish. It's a healthier alternative that still tastes like an indulgence. *Serves 8*

Position an oven rack in the center of the oven and preheat the oven to 375°F.

for the filling: In a medium bowl, combine the peaches, blueberries, maple syrup, vanilla, cinnamon, lemon zest, lemon juice, and salt. Pour into a 9-inch square baking dish.

for the topping: In a medium bowl, combine the almonds, oats, honey, safflower oil, and cinnamon. Stir until well combined.

Sprinkle the topping evenly over the filling. Bake until the topping is browned and the filling is bubbling, 30 to 35 minutes.

Let cool for at least 30 minutes before serving.

⅔ cup Cashew Cream (recipe follows)

2 cups (12 ounces) 41% cocoa vegan chocolate chips

1 teaspoon light agave nectar

1 teaspoon pure vanilla extract

Grated zest of ½ medium orange

per truffle: Calories 52; Protein 1g; Carbohydrates 6g; Dietary Fiber 1g; Sugar 0g; Total Fat 3g; Saturated Fat 1g; Sodium 0mg

vegan chocolate truffles

Vegan chocolate has no milk solids in it; sometimes it has a little coconut. You can buy it at Whole Foods or any natural foods store. Cashew cream stands in for the heavy cream you'll find in regular truffles, contributing a great texture but no discernible flavor. Roll these in finely chopped pistachios or crystallized ginger or give them a final dusting of cocoa powder, if desired.

makes about 32 truffles

In a medium, heat-proof bowl, combine the cashew cream and chocolate chips. Set the bowl over a saucepan of barely simmering water. Stir occasionally until the chocolate has melted and the mixture is smooth, about 2 minutes. Remove the bowl from the heat and whisk in the agave, vanilla, and orange zest. Refrigerate the mixture until firm, about 1 hour.

With a 1-tablespoon round measuring spoon, scoop out the mixture onto a baking sheet lined with parchment paper. With damp hands, roll the scoops into balls and return to the baking sheet. Refrigerate until firm, at least 1 hour, or for up to 2 weeks before serving.

cashew cream

You need only ⅔ cup of this to make the truffles, but you can't blend that little. So either make a double batch of chocolates or sweeten leftover cashew cream with agave or sugar and use it to top cakes, ice cream, or coffee drinks.

MAKES 1⅓ CUPS

1 cup unsalted raw cashews

Soak the cashews in 1 cup water for at least 2 hours or overnight at room temperature. In a blender, mix the cashews and water at high speed until creamy, about 1 minute.

sugar fixes

We all get them, whether at 4 p.m. or before bed. I've found that the best way to deal with a sugar craving is with something frozen that takes a while to melt in your mouth. That way you can savor the sweetness longer. Here are my top five things to freeze so I'm ready no matter when my sweet tooth rears its head:

- **CHOCOLATE CHIPS**

- **GRAPES**

- **MINI PEPPERMINT PATTIES**

- **SLICED BANANA** (I freeze them in zip-top baggies)

- **BERRIES**

If my frozen stash is depleted, I go for:

- **APPLE SLICES** sprinkled with ground cinnamon

- **BERRIES DRIZZLED** with light agave nectar or honey

- Any of the **FROZEN SMOOTHIES** in the Juices & Smoothies chapter (see page 52)

½ cup sugar

1½ packed cups fresh mint leaves

1 (2½- to 3-pound) cantaloupe, peeled, seeded, and cut into 1-inch pieces (4 cups)

3 tablespoons fresh lime juice (from about 3 large limes)

per serving: Calories 161; Protein 2g; Carbohydrates 41g; Dietary Fiber 2g; Sugar 37g; Total Fat 1g; Saturated Fat 0g; Sodium 17mg

cantaloupe and mint granita

This is so refreshing and makes a lovely, light palate cleanser after dinner. The flavors are sophisticated but kids love this, too. Jade likes to scrape off the flecks of flavored ice to make "snow cones." *serves 4*

In a small saucepan, combine 1 cup water, the sugar, and 1 cup of the mint leaves over medium heat. Bring to a boil, reduce the heat, and simmer, stirring occasionally, until the sugar has dissolved, about 5 minutes. Remove the pan from the heat and allow the syrup to cool, about 20 minutes. Strain before using.

In a blender, puree the cooled syrup, cantaloupe, and lime juice until smooth. Add the remaining ½ cup mint leaves and blend until finely chopped. Pour the mixture into a 9 x 13-inch glass baking dish and freeze until firm, at least 8 hours or overnight.

Use the tines of a fork to scrape the granita into chilled bowls and serve.

14 ounces dried Mission figs, stemmed and coarsely chopped (3 cups)

2 tablespoons unsalted creamy almond butter

1 cup (6 ounces) 41% cocoa vegan chocolate chips

2 teaspoons coconut, safflower, or grapeseed oil

¾ teaspoon flaky sea salt, such as Maldon

per bite: Calories 56; Protein 1g; Carbohydrates 10g; Dietary Fiber 2g; Sugar 6g; Total Fat 2g; Saturated Fat 1g; Sodium 53mg

chocolate fig bites

This is my favorite go-to dessert—it's like a bonbon, but better! These bites are chewy, decadent, and sweet because of the figs. And, who doesn't like something dipped in chocolate? The little hit of sea salt is the perfect contrast to the sweetness.

Makes 34 bites

Line a small baking sheet with parchment paper.

In a food processor, combine the figs, almond butter, and 2 tablespoons water. Blend until smooth, scraping down the sides of the bowl as needed with a rubber spatula. Using a 1-teaspoon measure, scoop the fig mixture and roll with your hands into 1-inch balls. Put the fig balls on the prepared baking sheet.

Put the chocolate chips and oil in a heat-proof medium bowl. Set the bowl over a small saucepan of barely simmering water and stir until the chocolate is melted and smooth, 2 to 3 minutes.

Using a fork, dip the fig balls in the melted chocolate to coat evenly, allowing any excess chocolate to drip back into the bowl. Return the fig bites to the baking sheet and sprinkle with the salt. Refrigerate until the chocolate has set, about 30 minutes. Store covered in the refrigerator for up to a week.

CHOCOLATE FIG BITES, PAGE 231, AND
SPICED PUMPKIN-RAISIN COOKIES

1 cup all-purpose flour

⅔ cup old-fashioned rolled oats

1 teaspoon ground cinnamon

½ teaspoon baking soda

½ teaspoon fine sea salt

¼ teaspoon ground allspice

¾ cup raw sugar (such as Sugar in the Raw)

½ cup canned pumpkin puree

⅓ cup safflower or grapeseed oil

1 tablespoon pure maple syrup

1 teaspoon pure vanilla extract

½ cup raisins

per cookie: Calories 91; Protein 1g; Carbohydrates 15g; Dietary Fiber 1g; Sugar 9g; Total Fat 3g; Saturated Fat 0g; Sodium 70mg

spiced pumpkin-raisin cookies

I make these in the fall, and always at Halloween, because the colors and flavors match so well with the season. Jade devours these chewy cookies, which is always a great sign—especially for a vegan cookie! *Makes about 24 cookies*

Position a rack in the center of the oven and preheat the oven to 350°F. Line 2 large baking sheets with parchment paper.

In a medium bowl, stir together the flour, oats, cinnamon, baking soda, salt, and allspice. In a large bowl, whisk together the sugar, pumpkin puree, oil, maple syrup, and vanilla. Using a flexible rubber spatula, gradually stir the flour mixture into the pumpkin mixture. Stir in the raisins.

For each cookie, drop 1 generous tablespoon of batter onto a prepared sheet, spacing the mounds about 1 inch apart. (Or use a mini ice cream scoop.) Using moistened fingertips, flatten each to a 2-inch-diameter round.

Bake the cookies until browned around the edges and no longer sticky on top, 17 to 20 minutes. Using a metal spatula, transfer the cookies to a wire rack and cool completely.

½ cup almond flour

2 tablespoons brown rice flour

½ teaspoon baking powder

¼ teaspoon baking soda

1 teaspoon ground cinnamon

⅛ teaspoon fine sea salt

3 tablespoons safflower or grapeseed oil

3 tablespoons pure maple syrup

1 large egg, at room temperature

¼ cup grated carrot

¼ cup grated zucchini

¼ cup raisins

per muffin: Calories 68; Protein 1g; Carbohydrates 8g; Dietary Fiber 1g; Sugar 6g; Total Fat 4g; Saturated Fat 0g; Sodium 82mg

carrot and zucchini mini muffins

These are a tiny, sweet little pick-me-up. If we have leftovers, Jade knows this is the one cupcake she can eat for breakfast, too, making it a favorite in our house.

Makes 12 mini muffins

Position an oven rack in the center of the oven and preheat the oven to 350°F. Line 12 mini muffin cups with paper liners.

In a medium bowl, whisk together the almond flour, brown rice flour, baking powder, baking soda, cinnamon, and salt.

In a separate medium bowl, whisk together the oil, maple syrup, and egg. Add the flour mixture and stir until just combined. Mix in the carrot, zucchini, and raisins.

Using 2 small spoons, fill the prepared muffin cups three-quarters full with the batter. Bake until light golden, about 15 minutes. Let cool for 5 minutes in the pan. Transfer the muffins to a wire rack to cool completely, about 30 minutes.

1 cup honey

1 large egg, at room temperature

8 tablespoons (1 stick) unsalted butter, cut into ½-inch pieces, at room temperature

1 tablespoon pure vanilla extract

1 cup unsweetened dried cranberries, coarsely chopped

½ cup slivered almonds, toasted (see Cook's Note, page 116), coarsely chopped

3 cups crispy brown rice cereal, such as Nature's Path Crispy Rice

4 ounces dark chocolate, finely grated

per cookie: Calories 102; Protein 1g; Carbohydrates 14g; Dietary Fiber 1g; Sugar 8g; Total Fat 5g; Saturated Fat 2g; Sodium 3mg

chocolate cranberry treats

Brown rice cereal makes these taste like the crunchy, chewy, Rice Krispies treats I loved as a kid, except that these have the wonderful addition of chocolate! I use a Microplane zester to grate the chocolate. A couple of these as dessert at night and I go to bed happy. *makes about 36 cookies*

Line a baking sheet with wax paper.

In a 5-quart saucepan, whisk together the honey, egg, butter, and vanilla. Bring to a boil over medium heat. Reduce the heat and simmer, whisking regularly, for 15 minutes. Stir in the cranberries, almonds, and rice cereal until combined. Let the mixture cool in the pan for 45 minutes.

Put the grated chocolate in a small bowl.

With slightly damp hands, firmly press the rice mixture together into 36 balls, each about 1 inch in diameter. Roll the cookies in the chocolate until coated and place on the prepared baking sheet. Refrigerate until firm, about 1 hour or for up to 3 hours before serving.

1 pound medium strawberries, hulled and quartered

¼ cup fresh orange juice (from about 1 large orange)

2 tablespoons fresh lemon juice (from 1 large lemon)

2 tablespoons honey

1 cup blueberries

special equipment: Popsicle sticks and 1 or 2 ice cube trays

per pop: Calories 17; Protein 0g; Carbohydrates 4g; Dietary Fiber 1g; Sugar 4g; Total Fat 0g; Saturated Fat 0g; Sodium 1mg

strawberry and blueberry (ladybug) pops

These are red with dark blueberry spots that make them look like ladybugs. They are pure fruit with a little bit of honey to sweeten them. Fantastic on a hot day. *makes 22 pops*

In a blender, puree the strawberries, orange juice, lemon juice, and honey until smooth.

Pour the mixture into an ice cube tray, filling each cube three-quarters full. Push some blueberries into each ice cube cup. Freeze for 1 hour.

Insert a stick into each cup and freeze until firm, another 4 to 5 hours.

Twist the ice cube trays to remove the ice pops and serve.

1 cup brown rice flour

½ cup almond flour

½ cup unsweetened cocoa powder

½ teaspoon fine sea salt

½ teaspoon baking soda

½ teaspoon baking powder

½ cup safflower or grapeseed oil

½ cup unsweetened applesauce

¼ cup pure maple syrup

2 large eggs, at room temperature, beaten

1 teaspoon pure vanilla extract

1 (12-ounce) bag bittersweet chocolate chips

per muffin: Calories 331; Protein 5g; Carbohydrates 38g; Dietary Fiber 3g; Sugar 6g; Total Fat 20g; Saturated Fat 6g; Sodium 173mg

chocolate muffins

These are nice and moist and chocolaty and studded with chocolate chips—just like a good chocolate muffin should be—but I don't have to feel guilty about eating these before bed. Applesauce replaces the usual butter and maple syrup replaces the white sugar. *Makes 12 muffins*

Position an oven rack in the center of the oven and preheat the oven to 350°F. Line 12 muffin cups with paper liners.

In a medium bowl, whisk together the brown rice flour, almond flour, cocoa powder, salt, baking soda, and baking powder.

In a large bowl, whisk together the oil, applesauce, maple syrup, eggs, and vanilla until blended. Add the flour mixture and stir just until blended. Stir in the chocolate chips.

Using an ice cream scoop, scoop the batter into the muffin liners. Bake until the tops of the muffins crack and a cake tester or wooden skewer inserted into the center of the muffins comes out with moist crumbs attached, 25 minutes. Unmold and cool on a wire rack for at least 1 hour before serving.

1 cup brown rice flour

½ teaspoon baking soda

½ teaspoon fine sea salt

¼ teaspoon baking powder

¼ teaspoon ground cinnamon

½ teaspoon ground nutmeg

½ cup safflower or grapeseed oil

¼ cup pure maple syrup

2 large eggs, at room temperature, beaten

2 teaspoons pure vanilla extract

1 cup mashed banana (about 3 small bananas)

1 cup fresh blueberries

per muffin: Calories 184; Protein 2g; Carbohydrates 21g; Dietary Fiber 1g; Sugar 9g; Total Fat 10g; Saturated Fat 1g; Sodium 156mg

blueberry banana muffins

I adore banana muffins. Which is good, because when you have a five-year-old in the house, you've got a lot of bananas! To use them up before they go bad, this is now my go-to recipe. Blueberries add a little tartness to the mix. I make these after dinner, serve them warm out of the oven (our favorite way to eat them), and then enjoy leftovers at breakfast. *Makes 12 muffins*

Position an oven rack in the center of the oven and preheat the oven to 325°F. Line 12 muffin cups with paper liners.

In a medium bowl, whisk together the rice flour, baking soda, salt, baking powder, cinnamon, and nutmeg.

In a large bowl, whisk together the oil, maple syrup, eggs, and vanilla until blended. Stir in the bananas and blueberries. Add the flour mixture and stir until just blended.

Spoon ⅓ cup of the batter into each muffin liner. Bake until a cake tester or wooden skewer inserted into the center of the muffins comes out with moist crumbs attached, 25 to 30 minutes. Unmold and cool completely on a wire rack for at least 1 hour before serving.

rolls

1½ cups cooked rice noodles, cooled and drained

¼ cup honey

¼ packed cup fresh mint leaves, finely chopped

6 (8-inch) rice paper rounds

6 medium strawberries, hulled

6 tablespoons sliced almonds, toasted (see Cook's Note, page 116)

1 mango, peeled and cut into ¼-inch-thick slices

dipping sauce

¼ cup packed fresh mint leaves, finely chopped

¼ cup honey

¼ cup fresh lime juice (from 3 large limes)

per serving: Calories 249; Protein 3g; Carbohydrates 52g; Dietary Fiber 2g; Sugar 28g; Total Fat 5g; Saturated Fat 0g; Sodium 27mg

fruit spring rolls

This is one of my favorite things to serve when people come over in the summer. These pretty rolls transform your standard fruit plate into something special, a real treat for adults and kids alike. You can find the rice noodles, often labeled "Pad Thai Noodles," and the rice paper rounds in the Asian section of many grocery stores. *serves 6*

for the rolls: In a medium bowl, toss the noodles, honey, and mint using 2 forks. Lay a damp kitchen or paper towel on a counter. Soak a rice paper round in warm water until softened, 20 to 30 seconds. Put the rice paper on the damp towel. Spoon ¼ cup of the noodle mixture in the center of the rice paper and form into a 3 x 2-inch rectangle. Using a paring knife, slice a strawberry lengthwise into ¼-inch slices. Arrange the slices over the noodle mixture. Sprinkle 1 tablespoon of the almonds on top. Arrange 2 to 3 mango slices on top of the almonds. Roll the rice paper around the filling and seal the ends with a little water. Repeat with the remaining ingredients. Wrap the finished spring rolls in damp paper towels and store in the refrigerator for up to 5 hours.

for the dipping sauce: In a small bowl, combine the mint, honey, and lime juice. Pour into a serving bowl.

Arrange the spring rolls on a platter and serve with the dipping sauce.

½ cup all-purpose flour

3 tablespoons almond flour

½ teaspoon baking powder

⅛ teaspoon baking soda

½ teaspoon ground cinnamon

¼ teaspoon fine sea salt

1 large egg

2 tablespoons frozen apple juice concentrate, thawed

2 tablespoons plain nonfat (0%) Greek yogurt

2 tablespoons safflower or grapeseed oil

½ teaspoon pure vanilla extract

⅓ cup grated carrot

3 tablespoons dried currants

6 tablespoons nonfat (0%) honey-flavored Greek yogurt

per cupcake: Calories 76; Protein 2g; Carbohydrates 9g; Dietary Fiber 1g; Sugar 4g; Total Fat 4g; Saturated Fat 0g; Sodium 83mg

mini carrot-apple cupcakes

I love using almond flour in these cupcakes, which have a great moist crumb and nutty flavor. They may not look "healthy," even though they are. Sometimes that's the secret to making a yummy dessert! *makes about 12 mini cupcakes*

Position an oven rack just below the center of the oven and preheat the oven to 350°F. Line 12 mini muffin cups with baking papers.

In a medium bowl, whisk together the flour, almond flour, baking powder, baking soda, cinnamon, and salt to blend.

In a large bowl, whisk together the egg, apple juice concentrate, yogurt, oil, and vanilla. Stir in the flour mixture and then stir in the carrot and currants.

Drop 1 tablespoon of batter into each paper liner so the liner is full. Bake the cupcakes until a toothpick inserted into a cupcake in the center (not the edge) comes out clean, about 12 minutes. Cool the cupcakes in the pan for 5 minutes. Then gently remove from the pan and transfer to a wire rack. Cool completely.

Top each cupcake with honey-flavored yogurt and serve.

1 cup brown rice flour

¼ cup coconut flour

½ teaspoon baking soda

½ teaspoon baking powder

½ teaspoon fine sea salt

½ cup safflower or grapeseed oil

¼ cup unsweetened applesauce

¼ cup honey

Grated zest of 1 large lemon

¼ cup fresh lemon juice (from 1 large lemon)

2 large eggs, at room temperature, beaten

½ teaspoon pure vanilla extract

1 cup unsweetened dried cranberries

per cookie: Calories 93; Protein 1g; Carbohydrates 11g; Dietary Fiber 1g; Sugar 4g; Total Fat 5g; Saturated Fat 1g; Sodium 85mg

cranberry-lemon cookies

This is an incredibly yummy citrusy cookie made without butter. These are great with a cup of tea or coffee at the end of a meal. All-fruit preserves would make a nice topping.

makes 24 cookies

Position an oven rack in the center of the oven and preheat the oven to 375°F. Line 2 baking sheets with parchment paper.

In a medium bowl, whisk together the brown rice flour, coconut flour, baking soda, baking powder, and salt.

In a large bowl, whisk together the oil, applesauce, honey, lemon zest, lemon juice, eggs, and vanilla until blended. Add the flour mixture and stir just until blended. Stir in the cranberries.

Using a 1-tablespoon measure, spoon batter onto the parchment. Using damp fingers, flatten each one into a ⅓-inch round. Bake until slightly golden on top, about 15 minutes. Cool on a wire rack for at least 1 hour before serving.

1 pound frozen blueberries, thawed and drained

⅓ cup plus 1 tablespoon honey

2 (3-inch-long) sprigs fresh thyme

2 cups plain low-fat (2%) Greek yogurt, cold

¼ cup light agave nectar

2 tablespoons fresh lemon juice (from 1 large lemon)

per serving: Calories 299; Protein 8g; Carbohydrates 64g; Dietary Fiber 3g; Sugar 59g; Total Fat 3g; Saturated Fat 2g; Sodium 63mg

blueberry frozen yogurt

This is everything frozen yogurt should be: sweet but a little tangy. And it has a beautiful deep lavender color. *Serves 4*

In a small, heavy saucepan, combine ¼ cup of the blueberries, 2 tablespoons water, 1 tablespoon of the honey, and the thyme sprigs. Using a fork or a potato masher, coarsely mash the blueberries. Bring to a boil over medium-high heat. Remove the pan from the heat, cover, and let the mixture stand for 15 minutes. Uncover the pan and let the syrup cool slightly. Discard the thyme sprigs.

In a blender or food processor, combine the remaining blueberries, the remaining ⅓ cup honey, the yogurt, agave, lemon juice, and the cooled syrup. Blend until the mixture is almost smooth.

Transfer the yogurt mixture to a glass container with a tight-fitting lid and freeze until the frozen yogurt firms up, at least 8 hours or overnight. The mixture will still be slightly soft.

Scoop the frozen yogurt into bowls and serve.

Vegetable oil cooking spray

6 tablespoons (¾ stick) unsalted butter

¾ cup semisweet chocolate chips

1 large egg

2 teaspoons pure vanilla extract

⅓ cup light agave nectar

Blueberry and Spinach Puree (recipe follows)

¼ cup brown rice flour

2 tablespoons flax meal

1 tablespoon unsweetened cocoa powder

¼ cup old-fashioned rolled oats, ground in a food processor

¼ teaspoon fine sea salt

per brownie: Calories 165; Protein 2g; Carbohydrates 19g; Dietary Fiber 2g; Sugar 14g; Total Fat 10g; Saturated Fat 6g; Sodium 52mg

chocolate blueberry brownies

These were inspired by my trip to St. Jude Children's Research hospital. The chef there made some super-yummy brownies— with blueberries and spinach! I came up with my own version using agave. These are moist, chocolaty, and just sweet enough. No one will ever know your healthy little secret.

makes 12 brownies

Preheat the oven to 350°F. Spray the bottom only (not the sides) of a 9-inch square baking pan with vegetable oil cooking spray.

Put the butter and chocolate chips in a heat-proof bowl. Set over a saucepan of barely simmering water. Stir until the butter and chocolate are melted. Set aside to cool.

Meanwhile, in another bowl, whisk together the egg, vanilla, agave, and blueberry and spinach puree. Stir in the cooled chocolate mixture.

In a mixing bowl, stir together the brown rice flour, flax meal, cocoa powder, oats, and salt. Add to the chocolate mixture and stir to combine; do not overmix. Pour the batter into the prepared pan. Bake until a cake tester or wooden skewer inserted into the center comes out clean, 25 to 30 minutes.

Allow to cool completely in the pan before cutting into 12 brownies. The brownies will keep, covered tightly, for up to a week in the refrigerator.

blueberry and spinach puree

MAKES ½ CUP

1¼ cups baby spinach

½ cup fresh or frozen blueberries, thawed and drained

½ teaspoon fresh lemon juice

Bring the spinach and 2 tablespoons water to a boil in a medium saucepan. Turn the heat down to low and simmer until the spinach is wilted and very tender, about 10 minutes. Set aside to cool for 10 minutes.

Combine the spinach, blueberries, and lemon juice in a food processor or blender. Process on high until smooth, stopping occasionally if necessary to scrape the sides. Add a little more water if necessary, to make a smooth puree.

things that make me happy

Sometimes it's the little things that bring so much joy. I like to keep fresh flowers in the house to bring the outdoors in. Orchids are fantastic because they stay in bloom for such a long time—often up to several months! Scented candles are another favorite, especially in flavors grapefruit, gardenia, and jasmine.

It's no secret that cooking for my friends and family makes me happy. When I can, I like to make lunch for Todd and surprise him at his office. He takes a break and we eat lunch together at his work.

And then there's my once-a-month girls' night, which I hold close to my heart. A few friends and I have a standing date. Sometimes we go out, but often we stay in and play board games or charades. We make it a potluck and everyone brings something. That way we can actually talk instead of shouting at each other in a noisy restaurant!

acknowledgments

Maybe it's the chef in me, but I like to think of this book as one long recipe for well-being, each part thought over, tested, and tasted in the hopes of being savored. And, just as with any good recipe, it takes a collection of carefully balanced ingredients, each one working to bring out the flavor of the next, to make a great dish.

Thanks to everyone who helped season this book:

To photographer Amy Neunsinger, for your meticulous eye, lovely energy, and inspiring connection to your lens; you and your team, Andy Mitchell and Hector Prida, make work an artist's playground for me. To my culinary testing delicious duo, Andy Sheen-Turner and Diana Bassett, for your patience, passion, and diligence to help me achieve "just right." For clean aprons, hot coffees, good advice, and bad jokes, Ashley Reed. To Jen Barguiarena and assistant Ian Hartman, for your visionary prop styling and ever so golden forks.

To the ladies who turn words into chocolate cake for me, Pam Krauss, Rica Allannic, Marysarah Quinn, Kate Tyler, and Anna Mintz at Clarkson Potter; your guidance (and grammar patrol) is so appreciated. Thank you to Marjorie Livingston for her nutritional wisdom.

A big thank-you to Carrie Purcell and assistant Beryl Cohen, for bringing your food styling prowess to make an ordinary grape absolutely "smolder." To Sandy and Nelson, for welcoming us to your table and letting us call it home for our shoot; you are so kind. To Julie Morgan, you are the salt to my pepper and I thank you for being so good at making a girl feel pretty with your beauty magic . . . even at 5 a.m.

For your continued dedication, support, and willingness to try new dishes: Jon Rosen, Suzanne Gluck, and Eric Greenspan. I am endlessly thankful to have you at my table.

To my family, thank you for keeping your hearts, your mouths, and our home open to every inspiration that comes my way. You are my true secret ingredients to making life so unbelievably delicious.

credits

Target	Table Art	Chantecaille	Jouer
Clairol	H.D. Buttercup	Koh Gen Doh	

index